Life of a Low Lady

Life of a Low Lady

– memoirs of a contralto

PAMELA BOWDEN

A Thames/Elkin Publication

First published 2002
A Thames/Elkin Publication
Distribution by William Elkin Music Services
Station Road, Salhouse
Norwich
Norfolk NR13 6NS

ISBN 0 903413 66 3

Type management by John Saunders

Printed and bound in the UK by
Thanet Press Ltd, Union Crescent, Margate, Kent CT9 1NU

Contents

Acknowledgements

MY MOST GRATEFUL THANKS to Tamar File who not only sings beautifully but types masterfully. She interpreted my handwriting, transformed these pages over many weeks of labour and did amazing things with the computer. I should have been lost without her. Profound thanks to Luisa Shannahan who gave generously and unstintingly of her time to read, comment and advise on each draft. She was rigorous in correcting my grammar and spotting inconsistencies, while remaining ever encouraging and supportive. Through it all she managed to keep our spirits up. Any remaining errors are entirely my fault.

Thanks to all my friends who have urged me on with enthusiasm and cries of 'When can we read it?'

Finally, thanks to my daughter and son

– to Michèle for her interest in learning about the extended family and about my life outside the home

– to Justin for the loan of his balcony in Muscat where much of this was written and for his genuine pleasure in reading the narrative as it progressed.

Photo credits: Isaac Berez, p85; Guy Gravett, pp120-121; Guttenberg, p6; Jamie Hodgson, p77; Houston Rogers, p77; Suzie Maeder, cover; Lotte Meitner-Graf, p52; Sport & General Press Agency, p87.

To Michèle and Justin, with all my love

Prologue

THE TITLE OF THIS BOOK arises from a joking reference to a few singers with whom a colleague kept in touch over the years. Among them were some contraltos, including myself, whom somebody once termed 'the low ladies'. I thought it both amusing and appropriate to use.

My apologies go to any casual reader who picks up the book, misled by its title into expecting it to contain lurid and sensational revelations. In such a case, please stop reading now. Nor for the student of singing is it yet another treatise on how to sing or train the voice. There are plenty of those on the market. Instead I have tried to paint a picture of a long and full life, to convey some of the vast changes that have occurred both to myself and those around me, and to give some flavour of the times that to most people today are in the realms of history.

To some readers the family history may not be of interest, but I assure them that it can easily be skipped.

Overture

IT WAS IN THE MILLENNIUM YEAR that I spotted, for the first time, the grim reaper peering over the horizon. Not perhaps surprisingly, you may think, since in this year I also reached my 75th birthday. I had from childhood held the hope that I would live to see the year 2000. To me, the 20th century was pictured as a kind of sloping path stretching away into the distance with each decade clearly marked out. The picture has always stopped at 2000, so that I now have to create a new image – something like breasting a hill and looking over the other side. I'm trying hard not to see this as downhill! Just now it seems as if I have turned around and am looking backwards at the crest.

What better moment therefore to think about jotting down some thoughts about my long and eventful life. This is primarily for the benefit of my grown-up children who, on the whole, know very little about the details of my childhood or my life and career before they were born. Somehow I never got around to talking much about myself, being married to a man who was an amusing raconteur, keeping the young ones – and our circle of friends – constantly entertained with his sometimes outrageous exploits and experiences. Mine seemed very much more tame and I tended to keep quiet about them at home – a fact which may astonish my various friends, colleagues and students. I don't think they look on me as a shrinking violet nor one who has to be persuaded to chatter.

Let me first say that some more welcome news from the doctors has pushed said grim reaper back over the horizon for the time being and things look a little rosier, but the urge to write it all down remains, so here goes.

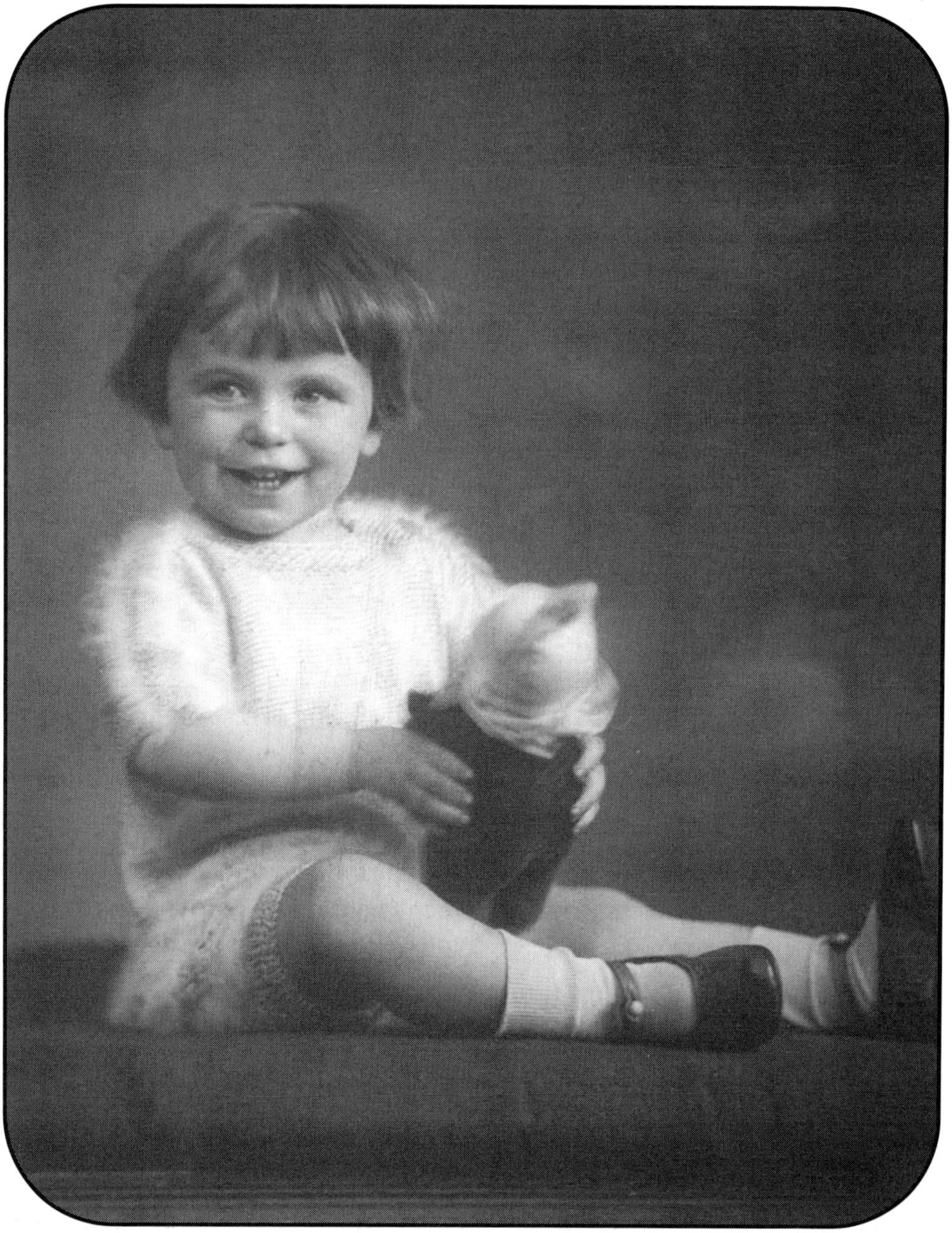

Pamela, aged 18 months

Act I, Scene 1
Beginners, Please

IT DOESN'T TAKE A MATHEMATICIAN to work out that I was born in 1925, on 17 April, just two days after my father's twenty-fourth birthday. Being both Arians it could be predicted that sparks would fly. My parents were from very different backgrounds, my mother having spent her life thus far in the south of England and my father a northerner from Lancashire. The maternal grandparents, William and Alice Gubbin, had been brought up in Launceston on the borders of Devon and Cornwall – they both spoke with a delightful, very slight west country burr – grandpa had been a master butcher. Surprisingly he retired very young and they moved to Kent in the early part of the century to live in a beautiful country house in the village of Cowden called Scarletts. I thought this was a romantic name and never tired of my mother's stories of growing up there with her two sisters, Winifred the eldest, Muriel the third in age and brother Kenneth the youngest. My mother Gladys hated her name and wanted to change it, at one time in her teens calling herself by the Welsh equivalent Gwladys, but that didn't last, thank goodness. They all seemed to spend idyllic summer days boating on the lake, in constant danger of frightening the swans and having limbs broken by their strong beaks and wings, as once happened. This made me wary of swans for ever. It can't have been all idyllic, as they must have been there during the First World War – but luckily for the family, grandpa was too old and Uncle Ken too young to be in the armed forces.

Meanwhile my father Bernard Coates Bowden was growing up in the small town of Littleborough, tucked under the Pennines and not far from the Yorkshire border. My Bowden grandparents, Harry and Bertha, lived in a fairly large square stone house called Mona Cliffe, perched above the road leading from the town up on to the moors. The front entrance was reached by an iron gate to a steep flight of steps up to the garden and a gravel path to the front door. In the middle of the lawn grew an ancient weeping willow under which I loved to hide and play as a small child. Nobody used the front entrance, though, and a lane around the back of the house led to the garages and rear entrance, so we always drove up that way.

Behind the house were farm lands and small houses and cottages in a little enclave. Further away was the golf club where my grandparents were leading lights, both of them playing to low handicaps and often winning trophies – as did my father later on. I never took to the game in spite of being encouraged to walk around the course with them – it seemed to me to be a cold and windy, rather miserable way of taking one's pleasure. Even then I preferred to sit in the warm with a good book and could be completely lost in another world even in a roomful of people. I remember discovering the books of Edgar Allan Poe and being frozen with horror while the family and friends were talking around me.

The Bowden family owned a nearby dyeing and finishing works called the Grove Dyeing Company. It had been founded by my great-grandfather and during my childhood the chairman was grandpa, with my father later becoming managing director and company secretary, and his cousins Ernest, Arthur and Leslie as directors.

The young Bernard had been sent away to a minor public school in North Wales called Epworth College, where he acquired a lifetime distrust of the Welsh whom he accused of being devious. I have photos of him as a little boy dressed up in costume for dancing class, brandishing an Irish shillelagh – a fearsome black wooden club which I have to this day hanging by my front door to deter would-be attackers! He had a younger sister, Marjorie, who shared with him ginger hair and pale freckled skin. The Bowdens were a musical lot – grandpa played the piano quite well, rather loudly as he was going deaf, when I was taken to visit for Sunday lunch and tea. His brother, 'old' Uncle Arthur, had been an aspiring tenor who once went to live at Golders Green in London to seek fame and fortune, but alas this eluded him and he returned to work at the Grove for the rest of his life.

His son, Leslie, suffered all his life from a distressing stutter and sadly received little sympathy on the whole. He might have had more help these days, but at that time therapy of any sort was looked on with suspicion and there was a certain stigma attached to such a disability, as if the poor man were slightly sub-normal. I liked him, though, and we were always friendly. In later life he sometimes came to London and loved to take me to concerts. He was a devoted music lover, and I remember he introduced me to Elgar's First Symphony which he thought was one of his finest works. Leslie had a huge record collection that was his mainstay in his years of retirement in a bright apartment on the seafront at Southport.

I think it must have been just at the end of the 1914-18 war that my father went to the Royal Manchester College of Music to study piano with Frank Merrick. He would dearly have loved to make a career as a concert pianist but unfortunately his studies were interrupted by a bout of ill-health. I never discovered exactly what was wrong but I suspect it was some form of nervous disability. He was always very highly-strung and easily upset, so it seems most likely that his music studies became too much for him and the doctor advised that he should lead an open-air life, less prone to stress. Consequently he was sent to Loughborough Agricultural College for a year and then my grandfather funded him first as a pupil on a farm and then with his own small farm in Kent. Fate decided that very soon he met my mother at a young farmers' dance, and within a very short time, they were married on 17 June 1924 in East Grinstead, with the reception at the Felbridge Hotel which still exists today though much modernised.

Within a few weeks I was on the way and the young couple realised there was not really any viable future for Bernard in farming. There was a place waiting for him at Grove Dyeing Company and they moved up to Littleborough – much against my mother's wishes, I suspect. Sadly she was never really happy 'up north'. She missed her family, the soft countryside of Kent and Surrey, the warmer, sunnier climate and the whole southern way of life. To her, Lancashire was dark and dreary, the weather wet and cold, and the people quite incomprehensible. She found the strong accents of the Grove workpeople and the local shopkeepers almost impossible to understand at first. She was in her mid-twenties, a bright, vivacious young woman who loved to have fun and go to parties. She was not quite a 'flapper' but certainly of that era and she enjoyed all the shows and popular music of the day. It must have been a dreadful shock to face not only the complete cultural change but also to be a young mother having to cope very suddenly with domesticity and the responsibility of a baby.

To crown it all, she and my grandmother did not get on well. Grandma was something of a martinet. In looks she resembled Queen Mary, wife of King George V, with the same wavy iron-grey hair drawn back into a bun, and the same inflexible upright carriage. She dressed beautifully, with impeccable taste, and everything on her person and in her house had to be of the finest quality. No expense was spared and my mother used to make fun of her favourite saying about a recent purchase – 'It's a good one', meaning it was

My father, Bernard Bowden, as Mayor of Rochdale in later life

expensive. Grandma cooked a wonderful Sunday roast and her gravy was legendary. She let me watch her prepare lunch – and in turn I am known for my gravy!

Mona Cliffe was a solid but elegant house, beautifully (and expensively) furnished. There were three large reception rooms – dining room, drawing room and morning room, which had glass double doors from the hall and a conservatory leading off it into the garden. On Sundays we were always in the drawing room, but on holidays such as Christmas when all the family were gathered together the fires were lit in the morning room too and we would open our presents in there and have morning coffee and later, sherry and aperitifs. The roaring coal fires were a feature of those days and I loved to sit watching the flames making pictures. The rest of the ground floor had a butler's pantry – though never a butler – in which grandma kept all her best silver and china, a big kitchen, scullery and store-room. There was a mysterious door to the cellar, down whose stone steps I was only allowed to go very rarely, usually with grandpa to bring up a bottle of wine or refill the coal scuttle from the coal cellar. In those days coal was delivered by a flat-topped lorry piled with one-hundredweight sacks that were emptied by tipping them down a chute at street level into each house's coal cellar – a dusty, dirty procedure. The coal men wore hessian ankle-length aprons and an empty sack around their shoulders on which to balance the coal sacks as they heaved them off the lorries. Invariably they wore caps with the peaks at the back – like today's young boys. They were totally black from the coal dust, with shiny white teeth and eyes. I loved to be given the job of counting the sacks to make sure we weren't being cheated as it was a well-known story that the men were on the lookout for an opportunity to keep the odd sack for themselves. If you had a big house you might have at least a ton, or twenty sacks, delivered at a time. The smaller, terrace houses had coal sheds or bunkers at the back instead.

As time went on and clean-air policies were introduced, householders had to find cleaner, smokeless fuel, before central heating became more widely available. The air over the industrial towns and cities was gradually cleaned up, as were the blackened buildings. The skies became clear and the whole atmosphere cannot now be compared with the 1920s and 1930s – though sadly pollution still affects us. But that's another story.

Our first family home was a terrace house in a crescent, Durn Lea, which curled away from the main road leading to the Grove and on towards Hebden Bridge and Yorkshire, following the curves of the valley. The dyeing business needed, as did the cotton mills, the soft water that ran off the hills where, in our case, it collected in a small reservoir. There were a number of buildings making up the dyeworks, not just one large multi-story like the cotton mills, and to my eyes it looked very untidy, with its uncoordinated roof shapes of all sizes. The office block was a neat square affair with a large general office and the chairman's (grandpa's) special office dominated by a vast mahogany desk. There was an enormous safe opened by a huge key kept in a secret place.

My father would sometimes take me to visit the machine shops where great bales of heavy cotton drill were being unrolled across moving beds of rollers, through vats of khaki or navy blue dye to the drying and shrinking areas. My great grandfather was distinguished by having invented a method of fast-dyeing khaki drill which was then becoming widely used by the army, and the firm owed its prosperity to government contracts to supply the army and navy with cloth for its uniforms. They also had one of the first machines that gave the name of 'Sanforized Shrunk' to the cloth. Between the wars this was not the only source of work, and many other types of material and shades were dyed, but during the Second World War production was completely given over to government war contracts. There was always a nasty smell permeating the whole works from the finishing process that used size and other chemicals. The noise in the machine shops was very loud indeed and the workers learned to lip-read and communicated by simple hand signals; no such things as ear-muffs in those days.

As an example of their way of speech, I remember one man, when being told he had to work a special shift, asking my father 'Shall uz bring uz dinners?'. They were a hard-working and loyal work force, many of whom stayed at Grove all their lives; the older ones had started with grandpa. It was very sad when, in the 1950s, the cotton trade went into decline. The former empire countries of India and Africa started their own spinning, weaving and dyeing industries, and with the armed forces being reduced to peace-time levels, our markets melted away. Some local mills were far-seeing enough to adapt to manufacturing the new man-made fibres – nylon and so on – and they went on to modernise and find new prosperity. At The Grove, all the family members were getting older. Because the Bowdens all had daughters and no sons, there was nobody to take their places. My father would secretly have liked me to take over but I couldn't have been less interested in running a factory. Therefore the decision was made to accept an offer from the government, made to the whole cotton industry, to give some degree of compensation to struggling mills that decided to give up the fight and close down. The Grove did just that and, along with the remaining cousins, my father took early retirement. A rather sad end to an era and three generations' heritage.

WHEN I WAS FOUR we moved to Rochdale, about five miles away. I now think my mother wanted to put some space between us and the grandparents and the works. We went to live in a small modern semi-detached house just outside the centre of the town. Nearby was a patch of waste land, or common land, which was just called the Common, where we local children used to play. We would run wild, climbing up tiny hills and jumping down vast distances of at least two feet. Another story goes that my mother once looked out of the window to see her little precious parading down the road with a net curtain pinned to her hair, the bride, with several other children walking behind holding up the curtain like a train. I must have been a proper little madam.

During that time I contracted what was much later diagnosed as a type of non-febrile rheumatic fever. I suffered severe pains in my hands and feet that everybody said were 'growing pains' and, of course, nothing was done. It left me with a heart-murmur, which again was not diagnosed until I had a medical examination for the forces during the war. The doctor said I was quite fit for service, and commented, 'It will either kill or cure you.' It did neither, of course.

MY GREAT-GRANDMOTHER died when I was seven. I remember meeting her only once, though we must have visited more often. She was a very old lady with a black velvet ribbon around her throat, and I think a white lace cap on her head – though that may be imagination. She was the mother of grandma Bowden and widow of Jarvis Coates, a builder. She lived in the house he had built for them. Many streets around the area had been built by him, one called Jarvis Street. My father inherited the house and we went to live there. It was a square house, shaped much like the type of house every child draws, with front door, a window on either side and three windows upstairs. The front garden was a steep rockery with steps leading up to the front door. It was at the end of a row of houses which apart from ours were large semi-detached.

Quite soon after moving there I met Eileen Curl who was to become my oldest and best friend. She was three years older than me – a lot at that age – but we became firm friends. I think she was quite young for her age and I was certainly considered old for mine, so it worked well. We became inseparable, her family living just down an unmade, gated road nearby called Bentmeadows. Many roads had curious names and I never ceased to be embarrassed by the name of the road where I lived. It was called Mizzy Road, and was a great source of mirth and teasing by my south country cousins. Goodness knows where the name came from and I would have dearly loved to change it. Opposite the house was a very big common, a large open space with nothing but a few sparse trees, and opposite, just to one side of our house, was a primary school called Cronkeyshaw School. The common was Cronkeyshaw Common.

On the far side of the common was a network of narrow cobbled streets of terraced houses or cottages probably built by Jarvis Coates, mostly 'two up and two down' with doorways on to the pavements and immaculately clean steps, adorned with various shades of donkey-stone – the pride and joy of the housewives. On one corner was a pie-shop. There they sold the most delicious home-made pies, and sometimes my mother would send me to buy pies for lunch. You could either have the gravy poured onto the pie or take some home in a jug. They invariably had meat and potato fillings, and the smell was enticing. There were little local grocery and greengrocery shops too but for her big shopping, mother would go to town where there was a good choice of shops and especially a quality grocers, Duckworth's, with a large premises beside a pedestrian lane called The Walk.

Nearer home was an establishment in Toad Lane, (a corruption of T'Owd – The Old Lane) now famous for being the site of the original Pioneers Society, the first Co-op shop ever. They started the system of giving discounts to shoppers and each time you made purchases you were given stamps to stick into a special book. After it was full you could redeem it for cash, and I was often allowed to go and collect the 'divi' and even keep it for myself. It was a nice walk from home into town, over the common, down into Heights Lane with its large houses on either side, and on, ever downhill, down Toad Lane and into the town centre. There were buses, of course, which ran down the cobbled roads on the far side of the common. They were hell for smart ladies with high heels like my mother, and much later, myself.

On Sundays when we were not going to Mona Cliffe for lunch and/or tea, I would go with Eileen and her younger brother Bob to the local Baptist church. I had been christened into the Church of England as a baby at the Littleborough Parish Church, by the vicar. Another story goes that one day he was being entertained to tea when I, aged about two, ran into the room declaring 'Mummy, the damned fire's gone out'. Collective embarrassment followed at what was then a serious swear-word, but later much laughter. Another family saying had come into being. So I was not, like Eileen and Bob, a non-conformist by upbringing, but I did enjoy going with them to the Sunday school. Occasionally we were taken from the schoolroom into the church for some service, perhaps very occasionally a baptism, where boys and girls in white robes were totally immersed in a deep bath in front of the pews. I wasn't very keen on this personally and was thankful I didn't have to undergo the ceremony. By far the most thrilling thing for me was to stand beside my teacher and hear her sing the hymns. She had the most beautiful voice – or so it seemed to me then – big, warm and vibrant. It was the first time I heard a really good voice and I was entranced. Perhaps that laid the foundation for my love of singing – who knows?

As time went along Eileen and I graduated to being allowed to go to the swings on our own, then to having proper bicycles. Mother bought my first beauty for me out of her own money, saved from the housekeeping, as Father had said he couldn't afford one. We used to cycle for miles, up into the countryside where one of our friends lived in a big, lonely house in the hills, and to the Syke Ponds where we'd fish for tiddlers and bring them home in jam jars. Another favourite haunt was Healey Dell, a local beauty spot. The lane leading down into the dell went past a tall cracked, discoloured brick wall behind which was a small reservoir. I was terrified and went past it as quickly as possible, either on my bike or walking, as I was sure it would collapse at any moment. The dell was a paradise for children and we would explore, play hide and seek, pick wild flowers that grew in profusion, and go blackberrying in the late summer.

A winter attraction was the local roller-skating rink run by an expert skater whom we nicknamed The Big Stiff after a comic paper character. I never had the courage to learn to skate well, although I longed to join my braver friends who used to dance to recorded music on Saturday afternoons. I had my own pair of splendid skates with shiny ballbearings in the wheels – but unluckily they didn't help me to spin around and skate backwards.

In our teens we would spend many summer hours at weekends and holidays at the open-air pool called, optimistically, The Riviera. There we congregated to flirt with the boys, have fun in the pool and enjoy whatever sunshine there was. It now seems that there were many sunny days – but in truth the weather was probably as variable and unreliable as now. We played tennis at the local club when allowed to and later joined as members.

In the very early years my schooling seemed ill-fated. The first preparatory school was a small establishment in the centre of the town called Hamer House School. It was run by two elderly ladies – perhaps they weren't so very old, but at the time they seemed so to me. It was a friendly, well run little school at which I made friends who were to remain so for many years to come. I was a bossy child and liked to rule the roost. At the end of the first day, my mother arrived to collect me and found me tying the shoe laces of a little boy called Tom Oldham. He grew up to become an oil executive out in Malaya and married a German wife. His mother had a dominant personality but was very kind-hearted. She liked me and would secretly have wanted me as a daughter-in-law one day, but that was never on the cards.

Another little boy called Victor Hoyle, later known as Tom, was very handsome and all us little girls wanted to be his special friend. He continued to win hearts all through his school days and on into adulthood – and for all I know may be doing so still.

Hamer House closed down after about two years due to the retirement of our lady head teacher, so I was next sent to St Elwyn's College, a grand name for another private prep school. This time it was situated in the suburb of Bamford in a large, attractive white house with its own grounds. There I stayed until age ten, when it too closed its doors this time due to the serious illness of the headmistress.

AS AN ONLY CHILD I was taken everywhere with my parents and spent a great deal of time in grown-up company, which perhaps accounts for the fact that I was precocious and more accustomed to adult conversation than childrens' play. This also made me unable to relate easily to my fellow pupils at school who regarded me as 'stuck-up' and, because I was bright, as 'teacher's pet'. I did my very best *not* to live up to this view of myself and tried very hard to be easy and friendly, but with only partial success throughout the school-days. There were, of course, some close friends, one of whom was Betty, a fat girl who used to be cruelly teased about her size. I liked her, though, and we visited each other's homes. One day Betty said it was her daddy's birthday, he was forty-eight. Not to be outdone I said 'So's my daddy'. I'll never forget my parents' mirth on being told of this – daddy was actually in his early thirties.

Because of the early demise of the school I was cast upon the educational scene at ten – and entry to the grammar schools was at age eleven. My father made urgent representations to the local education department to allow me to enter a year early. My exam results were good and I could easily fit into a class of eleven-year-olds. However, the Director of Education was adamant and would on no account allow me to go to the Rochdale High School for Girls, which was only five minutes walk from home and where my friend Eileen was already a pupil. My father was furious at such inflexibility but had to accept the decision. Boarding school was offered to me – Malvern or Cheltenham Ladies' Colleges among the suggestions – but I refused firmly as I didn't want to leave home.

I was eventually accepted by Heywood Grammar School. This was in a neighbouring town between Rochdale and Manchester, and involved a long and tedious journey by train and bus. I got used to it and in the summer would sometimes cycle by a route that avoided both town centres. I always enjoyed the school work; we had classes of some 32 boys and girls, with specialist masters and mistresses for each subject. The school was well equipped with a large assembly hall where we all gathered each morning for prayers and a hymn before classes started, and excellent science labs. A few teachers stand out in the memory: the music teacher, Rachel Pearson, who greatly encouraged me in my interest; Mr Hope, the physics master, whom we nicknamed Soapy and who had a crush on my mother, following her around on parents' evenings, much to our amusement; Mr Corlett (Corky), the chemistry master, a brilliant scientist but hopeless teacher as he couldn't bring himself down to our level; the headmaster Mr Oldroyd who persistently mispronounced my name, which came out as Pameela Boughdon; our English teacher Miss Evans who was passionate about her subject, especially Shakespeare, and made us learn great chunks of text from memory – wonderful mental discipline. She had an oddly posh way of speaking and used to say 'He that hath yahs to hyah, let him hyah'!! ('He that hath ears to hear, let him hear.') Lastly there was a dragon of a domestic science and sewing teacher who would not make any concessions towards my left-handedness and insisted on my using the right hand to sew hems and to embroider. She declared that the stitches sloped the wrong way with a left-hander. Thank God my other teachers had been more enlightened and I was never forced to write with my right hand.

I usually came near the top of the class but there was one boy I never managed to beat, except in French where I excelled. His name was Charles Booth. After school we lost touch and only about three years ago I came across his obituary in the *Daily Telegraph*. He had had a distinguished career in the Foreign Office, serving in the Far East for many years. I wrote to his widow offering condolences and saying that she would not know me but that Charles and I had been at school together. She wrote a charming letter back, telling me that Charles had been well aware of my career as a singer and she said he always attributed his love of opera to the fact that I had introduced him to it. Amazing. How I wish we had got in touch years earlier.

IN THE END, I took my School Certificate exams at 15, receiving nine credits and one distinction in French. I stayed on one more year at school to take Intermediate Higher exams in four subjects – English language, English literature, History and French. But by this time I was getting tired of academic study and didn't want to stay on for Higher Certificate and then university, although my teachers were keen for me to do so.

My love of music had grown and been fostered over the years. I started piano lessons at five and continued throughout the years with an excellent local teacher. At the same time my father had resumed piano lessons with the best-known local celebrity called George Whittaker. He was also a composer and I still have some of his songs in manuscript – and very good they were, with complex piano accompaniments, as might be expected. As a small child I used to lie in bed and listen to my parents playing, sometimes piano duets. My mother had a wonderful talent for playing by ear – she would listen to a popular song on the radio and be able to play it perfectly with all the right harmony. She had a pretty singing voice too, and they started to compose songs together, words by mother and music by father. They were quite melodious, and they had some published – but they did not persevere and later lost interest.

My mother had a violin that she played excruciatingly – whenever she picked it up, our dog howled piteously so she laughingly admitted defeat and put it away for ever. They had some other musical friends – one in particular had a fine baritone voice with a penchant for jolly, rollicking ballads and sea shanties. I loved those evenings and joined in whenever possible.

PERHAPS IT IS TIME NOW to talk about my mother's family and their influences on my early life. As I mentioned earlier, she was never really happy with her life in the north and I quickly picked this up from her even as a small child. It must be said that I was very close to her and never felt the usual girl's attachment to the father. He and I were too alike and knew only too well how to aggravate each other. It was always to my mother I turned for love and comfort – although I'm sure father did love me in his undemonstrative way. So, strongly influenced by mother's own preferences, I too felt the attraction of the softer countryside and climate of the south. Not only that, here lived my beloved aunt Muriel whom I adored and who showered me with love and attention. She was only eighteen when I was born and over the years we were devoted to one another. She put up with my moods and tantrums with unfailing good humour and a huge sense of fun. When the two sisters were together the house rang with laughter and giggles. At some silly comment they would laugh till they cried, and the rest of us joined in too. Life was indeed much more fun when she was around and it was great to see mother able to let herself go and enjoy being her real exuberant, high-spirited self.

Auntie Win was a little more serious, but she sometimes joined in the fun and one could see what a happy and secure upbringing the three of them had enjoyed, with their young brother Ken who they all said was spoiled because he was the only boy. Auntie Win had married a very wealthy man, heir to a big south London metal-box company and the cherished only son of Henry Francis, a man of great character who dominated the family.

The first house I remember in which they lived in style was called Caberfeigh, a large white mansion set back from the road linking Reigate and Redhill in Surrey. By then our grandparents and Muriel were living at Blackborough Lodge, just down the road, having lived in Lingfield for a short time after leaving Scarletts. The Francis household consisted of Henry, his son Leslie married to Auntie Win and their three children, Yvonne, Roger and Alan – known always as Jimmy since old Henry insisted on calling him Sonny Jim. Our ages came at two year intervals – Yvonne four years older than me, Roger two years older and Jimmy two years younger. The house was run by a rather splendid butler – who wore white gloves to supervise the dinner table – a cook/housekeeper, a couple of maids, gardeners and a chauffeur called Kemp who was with the family for years. His wife was the cook. They had to have the chauffeur because Henry couldn't (or wouldn't) drive, and poor Uncle Leslie suffered from quite severe epilepsy. I remember being horrified and frightened when I first saw him suffering a seizure. Today the condition would probably be better managed but then one never knew when he might turn deathly pale, drop to the floor and thrash about. Because of this affliction he was never able to work, but happily his father was able to support them all in great comfort.

Auntie Win was an elegant lady, slim like all three sisters but with the most beautiful ankles and slender legs – which we others envied. She had an extensive wardrobe and was very generous in handing on model clothes to her less well-off sisters. I well remember a Worth dress that she gave to mother which was both chic and very long-wearing. We children would play together in the nursery which had a splendid old rocking horse and a huge layout of Hornby railway which the little boys – and big boys – spent hours with. I learnt to ride a bike in their garden – there was a long stretch of lawn with a gentle slope ideal for the purpose and of course I learnt by the usual method of thinking Roger was still hanging on to me when in fact he had let go and I was riding on my own.

Another vividly recalled scene took place one afternoon when we were all in the drawing-room and the girls were gathered around the piano. Auntie Win was playing and she and Muriel were singing 'In her sweet little Alice-blue gown'. Towards the end they started to harmonise and when they finished, I was hugely impressed and said, to everyone's delight, 'Oh, Auntie you do sing so beautifully out of tune.'

At this time, Grandpa had set Uncle Ken up in a charming farm called The Old Mill near the little village of Chiddingstone in Kent. We children loved to visit there and we were allowed to use either a punt or a small dinghy to row up the stream as far as we could go before it became too overgrown to proceed. We called it 'going up the Amazon', and had great games. There was an old water-mill set over a weir with a huge water-wheel, where we had to be very careful because it could be dangerous. The floors in the mill, linked by rickety ladders, were not too safe but I loved the place with its dusty air and lingering smell of grain. We were allowed to feed the chickens and used to venture into the field containing the bull only with the elders who carried walking-sticks. I was terrified to wear anything red in case I was chased.

It was a magical time – there was not yet much traffic on the country lanes and we would help uncle to drive the cattle along from the fields into the barns for milking. Later on Ken married a lovely lady called Dorothy and I was sometimes invited to stay for a few days on my own. There was a prolific old wisteria laden with blossom growing against a wall and we would have tea beside it on hot summer days. The farmhouse was very old, with a polished oak staircase and stone floors. A huge inglenook in the living room was decorated with dozens of horse brasses, with shotguns hung on the walls – illegal today, of course. We would sometimes have jugged hare or a rabbit pie, and one had to be careful not to break a tooth on an overlooked piece of shot. Ken was at the farm during the war but soon afterwards the perennial problems of farming became too much for him, and he, Dorothy and their little girl Jill moved to South London, buying and running a greengrocery business. Later still, after Jill's marriage to a rising young business executive, John Vinnicombe, they sold up and went back to Kent, to live in Hildenborough, where Ken died in the 1970s of emphysema.

Jill and John had two children, Marcus and Gay (later to be known as Amanda). We used to visit from time to time and our elder children would play together – Marcus was a year older than my daughter Michèle – but we saw less of them when they moved up to Cheshire together with Dorothy, where they have remained. Marcus is now married with his own little daughter.

IN 1938 OUR SCHOOL took a group of the older children for a week or so to Paris. Although I was a year too young, the Head listened to my pleas and allowed me to go. I have for ever been grateful that I had this chance to see pre-war Paris. It was May and a magical time to see the boulevards, the parks and the famous sights. We stayed at a small hotel in the Latin Quarter –

itself an adventure – and visited the usual tourist venues, the Louvre, Notre Dame and others. Of course we went to the Eiffel Tower and there we saw a film crew working. When we asked who was in the film we were told Greta Garbo. We couldn't believe them and thought they were kidding. It was only a few months later we discovered it was perfectly true – the film was *Ninotchka* and indeed starred Garbo. We ate delicious cherries bought from street stalls, and visited an English tea room on the Rue de Rivoli where we ate little pastry boats filled with *crême patissière* and fruit. What lovely memories those were.

As an omen of things to come, Jewish refugees had come to live in Rochdale, among them Dr and Mrs Wertheimer, who became friends of my parents. He was obliged to retake his medical degree in order to practise in the UK, even though he had been highly qualified with a flourishing private practice in Vienna. They had fled with few possessions and I was very interested to observe their different and seemingly exotic way of life, their strange but delicious food and those melting vanilla *kipfeln* tasted for the first time. There was also another refugee family with a brother and sister, Kurt and Renate Scholl, with whom we became friendly.

Act I, Scene 2
Wartime

THEY SAY THAT EVERYONE REMEMBERS where they were when they heard the news of the assassination of President Kennedy. I believe people of my generation all remember where we were when we heard the news of the outbreak of war on Sunday 3 September 1939. We realised from that moment, listening to the radio in our sitting room at Moorlands, that nothing would be the same again. True, the effects of wartime restrictions took some time to bite. Apart from having to make blackout curtains for all the windows and there being no street lights at all, things went on much the same as ever. I went to school as usual on the first day of the new term in September and one of the younger children asked me what being at war meant. I remember replying that we would have to *fight*, that we might be invaded and that we were going to have a terrible time. Not too far from the truth. The months of the 'phony war', as they were called, ended with the Nazi invasion of France and the Netherlands, and then the evacuation of the army from Dunkirk. Little did I know then that my future husband was one of the thousands on the beach to be rescued by one of the small boats which so gallantly braved the aerial bombardment and the many hazardous crossings of the Channel.

I was fourteen in 1939. My parents suggested sending me over to our relatives in Vancouver, Canada.

(Just before the First World War, my maternal grandmother's sister Emma (*née* Dennis) followed her husband William Brendon and his brother Arthur in emigrating to Vancouver, Canada. Emma was accompanied by her small daughter Amy, my mother's first cousin. They soon established a thriving real-estate business but Emma was widowed within two years. The family 'went forth and multiplied' and now there is a large clan of relatives in and around Vancouver and British Columbia.

Amy married and had a daughter Joyce, who is my exact contemporary and with whom I have become close in love and friendship. It is a pity that the chance of meeting all this family was missed in 1939/40, and that we had to wait another 40 years before making it out to Vancouver. Amy, a great traveller, letter-writer and philosopher, paid us several visits and never ceased to amaze us with her energy and zest for life, even into old age.

I missed, too, early acquaintance with the delights of the city of Vancouver, the coastline, the surrounding mountains and the breathtaking beauty of the nearby ski resorts such as Whistler. Joyce's daughter Barbara married Alan Fraser and has two children, Christiana and Derrick, who all visit me from time to time.)

I firmly refused the offer of Canada, saying I wanted to be here where the action was. Life continued much as usual in some ways, but growing food shortages and increasingly stringent rationing meant that my mother had to use great ingenuity to create appetising and nourishing meals. This came about gradually but it wasn't long before we had to make trips into the country to buy chickens and eggs, slightly illegally, from any farmers willing to sell. The butter ration dropped to two ounces per person per week, eked out by substitutes when possible. The meat ration was also meagre, but none of us suffered any health problems. At that time, milk was still delivered by pony and cart, with two large metal urns on the back. We would take our jugs out to have them filled from a tap at the base of the urn, and it was my joy as a child to be allowed to ride in the milk float and even drive the horse. There was an ice cream vendor who drove around in the summer months, an Italian called Ianussi – whose ice cream was the most delicious creamy custardy yellow and utterly splendid. We would sometimes take out cups or mugs to be filled and topped with heavenly strawberry or raspberry sauce. There were, of course, cones and wafers on sale but the big cupful was for the greedy ones.

At weekends (even before the war we had stopped going so often to Mona Cliffe) we could drive out – petrol ration permitting – to beauty spots like the Trough of Boland, and to picturesque country inns and hotels. Our companions on these outings were often my father's cousin Edith (sister of 'young' Arthur) and her husband, a handsome, elegant director of John Bright's, the biggest cotton mill in the area, named Fred Train. Fred drove a smart sporty Jaguar – one of the first models. We would take picnics in the summer and play cricket beside the stream that runs through the valley at Boland. The road along it was gated and involved many stops and starts, which had us leaping out of the car to open and shut the gates as we went along. In winter our drives out to Cheshire usually involved afternoon tea at a country hotel such as The Bells at Little Peover – another name causing mirth even though we knew it was pronounced Peever. They had a roaring log fire in the lounge on those winter Sunday afternoons; very welcoming.

In 1940 we were anxious about the Gubbin and Francis families who were living under the direct flight path of the German bombers and fighters heading from the south coast towards London. They wrote to us with stories of first-hand witness of the dog-fights during the Battle of Britain and saw many planes shot down. Later, we listened with horror to newsreel accounts of the London blitz and of all the death and destruction. We daily expected to become the targets of German bombers and would nightly hear them droning overhead on their way to bomb Liverpool and its docks. The nearest we came to such horrors was the short, sharp blitz on Manchester which caused much damage in the city, and sadly, one of its oldest and most historical districts, called The Shambles, became literally so and was completely demolished. When the air-raid sirens would sound – almost every night for a few months – my mother and I would at first cower on the cellar steps as this was supposed to be one of the safest places, while my father was out on duty as an Air Raid Warden. Later he became a Special Constable, a kind of volunteer part-time policeman, and was rewarded at the end of the war with an inscribed truncheon with colourful gilt and red lettering which now hangs alongside the shillelagh. He was too old to be called up early in the war and then was declared to be in a reserved occupation and not liable for military service. When it was clear that our town was unlikely to be a specific target, we became braver and sat out air-raids in the comfort of our living rooms.

Extracts from my diary, 1941

A teenager's view of the war and life in wartime

New Year's Day	Wonder what this next year will bring. They say it will be very hard for us. Poor old Manchester could not be more in ruins even after only two nights of 'blitz'. Greeks still advancing into Albania and [we] are knocking at the gates of Bardia in Libya . . . .
2 January	Raids on N.W. last night and Daddy had to go out on duty until about 2.30 am.
4 January	Daddy came home with news of great scarcity of meat – could not get any butter.

6 January	Hurrah! Bardia has fallen and the Italian soldiers surrendered on all sides – half-starved and miserable, poor blighters. We are going on to Tobruk. Raid on London last night.
8 January	Heard about new meat rationing – 1/- and 1/6 per person per week.
9 January	Had dreadful night – was paralysed with fear at planes' droning. 2 great bombs on Rochdale, 345 houses damaged.
12 January	London blitzed again. More German ports and bases bombed.
14 January	Lowest shipping losses this week for a long time, 5th lowest since the war. Portsmouth blitzed last night. More Italian prisoners taken. We shan't know what to do with them soon.
23 January	Hurrah! We captured Tobruk. Australian soldiers did good work. General Wavell is a marvel . . . .
13 February	Went to M/cr and got there in time to catch glimpses of the King and Queen as they passed. The crowds were terrific. It was supposed to be a close secret! They were touring the bombed area.
20 February	Non-aggression pact between Bulgaria and Turkey.
21 February	Germans streaming into Bulgaria in plain clothes. Everything very unsettled in the Near-East. Turkey announced faith in alliance with Britain.
22 February	Visit to the Polish Ballet at the Opera House, Manchester. The performance was wonderful and it was pathetic to see the Poles doing their national dances in an alien country while theirs is in desolation.
23 February	Musso made a speech today – quite typical of all his speeches – bombastic, but not very assured of Libya – deprecated losses and boosted German friendship.
7 March	Heard siren in Manchester and a terrific roar. A German bomber went over with three fighters after it. Heard later it had machine-gunned somewhere in Heywood, circled M/cr and dropped bombs at Heywood Aircraft Factory, killing quite a few. Luckily it was brought down and one of our boys saw a fighter do the Victory Roll.

10 March	Lease and Lend Bill has passed the House of Representatives and I think it is law now. I wish they could hurry a bit. They are going to send food to us as well as armaments.
11 March	The London Philharmonic played in Rochdale tonight – wish I could have gone. Sirens went at 8.45pm. Mum had to go on duty. Dreadful night – bombs and guns galore! All clear about 11pm. Sir Walford Davies died today – what a loss to the musical world. Our shipping losses heavy. Got 7 planes down in a raid on Portsmouth last night.
12 March	Raids all over the place. Heard that Ken Johnson and his West Indian Dance Orchestra had all been wiped out except for the drummer in the Café de Paris.
14 March	Mr Harriman arrived from America to supervise the progress of the Lease and Lend Bill. Hope things will speed up now. There is talk of our getting oranges from Spain. I hope they do, for I have almost forgotten what an orange tastes like.
19 March	Cheese is going to be rationed as well as preserves. Blitz on Hull last night.
21 March	Blitz on Plymouth last night.
27 March	Marvellous news! There has been a lightning revolution in Yugoslavia – the people who signed the Pact [Tri-Partite Pact with Germany and Italy] have all been imprisoned and the government resigned in favour of the 18 year old boy King Peter. There is great rejoicing there and it certainly is a big one in the eye for old Adolph.
30 March	Great naval engagement with the Italians. 5 big ships sunk.
31 March	Number sunk is now 7. The Italians are completely useless at sea (as everywhere). It seems that at one point they were firing at each other.
1 April	Clydebank damage is the worst in the country, so it must be dreadful. We have seized a lot of Axis ships in America, including the 'Normandy'.
2 April	We are advancing further in Abyssinia towards Addis

Ababa. The battle is to be called the Battle of Cape Matapan. We captured Asmara today.

3 April There are serious strikes in America which will probably hinder production for us. I bet it is the Fifth Column at work. Italians scuttled 2 more ships. That is 5 so far.

4 April Benghazi has fallen back to German and Italian troops. What a blow!! I nearly wept with chagrin when I heard.

6 April Addis Ababa fell to us today. Hooray! Germany declared war on Yugoslavia and Greece, and attacked across their frontiers. It has been revealed that we have an army in Greece ready to help and attack the Germans. Nice work.

9 April Germans captured Salonika today. Greek forces are trapped E. of that town. Mr. Churchill made a speech today. Did not sound very optimistic, yet not pessimistic. Said all depended on American help in Atlantic. Said victories in Abyssinia freed our troops to reinforce Libya – would not be easy to stop Germans getting to Egypt.

12 April The queues outside shops were dreadful. Not a cigarette is to be got. Bristol heavily raided last night. Casualties heavy. RAF bombed Germans as they advanced into Greece. Everybody has to register for cheese rations.

13 April Germans captured Derna and claim to have surrounded Tobruk and got Bardia.

14 April We are 'retreating according to plan' as usual in Greece. Daylight raid in N.W. of which we heard only the siren and a lone bomber machine-gunned Norden, near the 'Riviera' .

15 April I was on duty [fire-watching] and it was a beautiful night – but with plenty of gunfire and flashings. The all-clear went at 4.18. We repeated an enemy attack on Tobruk. We are retreating everywhere in the Balkans. Enemy lost 15 tanks, 300 men and 22 planes.

16 April Last tower of the Crystal Palace blown up to prevent enemy using it as a signpost. Last night enemy raids covered N. Ireland. Italians in Abyssinia negotiating with us for peace. Yugoslavia stopped fighting today.

17 April Very heavy raid on London with many casualties. Attack on

Tobruk and Solum repulsed and enemy lost 1000 men. Heavy fighting in Greece.

18 April The raid on London the worst raid of the war. Hit Christie's sale room, St Paul's, Chelsea Hospital, Guys Hospital and countless other places. Historic rooms and monuments have been destroyed besides many innocent lives.

19 April Allied retreat in Greece, while inflicting heaving losses on enemy. We shot down a great many German planes recently and we are nightly making heavy raids on Bremen, Hamburg, Kiel etc. An Axis plan for dropping captured British bombs on the Vatican has been revealed, and we have said that if Athens or Cairo are bombed we will bomb Rome systematically till the end of the war.

21 April The Germans have captured Mount Olympus. Celebrated Hitler's birthday last night by heavily raiding all N.W. Germany.

22 April We have bombarded Tripoli from the sea and blown it to blazes.

27 April The Germans have captured Athens. We have repelled attacks on Tobruk. Mr Churchill gave a wonderful speech tonight. It lasted 35 minutes.

29 April Could not do any work for thinking about this evening. Mum and I went at 7 o'clock to the Champnesss Hall. It was packed. The Hallé Orchestra was jolly fine. Malcolm Sargent conducted and Cyril Smith played Rachmaninoff's Concerto No. 2. It was very good. Lawrence Turner was 1st violinist and Haydn Rogerson – Tommy Matthews' brother-in-law – was 1st cellist.

We are evacuating Greece. Fought a wonderful rearguard action.

30 April Got some tomatoes – hurray!

4 May Raschid Ali, the usurper of Iraq, has forbidden our troops to go into Iraq and he has appealed to Germany.

5 May Last night we had heavy raids over Merseyside and we brought down 18 planes.

6 May About 12 planes down last night. Fighting is going on in

Iraq against Raschid Ali. Shipping losses very high for April – I suppose it is owing to the evacuation from Greece.

7 May More heavy raids. We seem to get them every night now. Marvellous record – 24 down. That makes over 708 for the first week in May.

8 May More planes down again last night. We are marching towards Baghdad.

9 May Still more raids. There was a terribly heavy raid on London with many casualties and lots of damage. Brought down 24. Our night fighters are wonderful.

12 May Very heavy raid on London. Westminster Abbey, the Houses of Parliament and many other places badly damaged. We raided all over Germany again causing much damage and many fires.

13 May Great news today. Rudolf Hess, the deputy of Hitler and one of the cruellest Nazis, has landed from a plane in Scotland and has been captured. I could hardly eat my breakfast for excitement.

15 May More speculation about Hess. Duff-Cooper is trying to make out that the Nazi organisation's collapsing – utter drivel!!

16 May In music today Miss Pearson made me sing my song for the girls – my knees simply knocked with fright! At dinner-time rushed to the market and joined a queue for biscuits – got 1/2 lb – and also 1/2 lb of brandy snaps and a bar of chocolate. Quite an achievement.

The French are letting German planes use Syrian air-bases against us – the skunks!

19 May Spent all dinner-time practising feverishly. The concert was a great success. They all liked my song. Had a great many compliments.

An American hospital ship has been sunk and it is feared that many doctors, nurses and ambulances, and Free French troops were lost.

20 May German troops in New Zealand uniforms have landed in Crete and most have been rounded up. They dropped by parachute.

21 May Hundreds more troops have been landed in Crete but we have accounted for them.

22 May More parachutists landed in Crete and tried to land from the sea. Heavy fighting is going on.

27 May Roosevelt made a long speech declaring America in a state of extreme crisis.

The Germans sunk HMS Hood by a lucky shot in the ammunition hold, but we got hot on the trail of the nearest German ship, the Bismarck – supposedly unsinkable, and we sunk it after a battle.

31 May The situation in Crete is desperate. The Americans have sent their first shipload of foodstuffs for us.

1 June Great sensation!! All clothing and materials are to be rationed from today. What a greeting for June! We evacuate Crete today.

3 June Iraq has surrendered and we have restored the rightful King.

4 June [in Reigate, Surrey] All day I don't think there was a minute when we couldn't see or hear planes – there were Spitfires and Hurricanes all over the place. Germans are pouring through Syria now and the French are preparing to defend it. They have been given permission by Germany to fight our ships. I don't think it will be long before we are at war with France. It does seem wicked.

10 June We are still advancing steadily in Syria and our advance units are within 20 miles of Damascus. The Californian factory that has been on strike has been forced to return to work after being taken over by US troops.

16 June Roosevelt has ordered all German consuls, clubs and everything German to be closed as they were being used as propaganda bases.

20 June There is something funny going on between Germany and Russia.

22 June Terrific news today. Germany has invaded Russia with Finland and Rumania!!! We are thrilled! We are sure that Hitler has cooked his own goose now. Mr Churchill made a speech at 9 o'clock – we are going to help Russia.

23 June German attack has been held nearly everywhere along the whole front. America supports us but does not seem so keen on helping Russia much because of their dislike of communism. In Syria we have reached the oil pipe-line.

24 June Germans have captured Brest-Litovsk. Free Poland is going to support Russia and trust that Russia will not want to keep their part of Poland after war. During the last 2 days over 118 German planes have been brought down in Russia and over 5000 men captured.

25 June Was thrilled when I got home to find a charming letter from Norman Allin to say he would be very pleased to accept me as a pupil. Was I excited!!

27 June Germans have broken through Red lines at one place with tanks and their parachutists have been wiped out. I wish we could invade them while they are busy with Russia.

29 June Heard most marvellous speech by Quentin Reynolds (American) in the form of a Talk to Dr Goebels – he said he had called G. to listen earlier today. If only we had more men like Q.R.! We listened with bated breath to his withering sarcasm and the wonderful praise of us and what we could do. Both sides are inflicting heavy casualties on each other and the numbers of planes and tanks destroyed are terrific – more German than Russian, though – but one really doesn't know what to believe with them both being incorrigeable liars! The Germans have launched a special communiqué at their people with much drama and effect – e.g. trumpet blowing and weird music.

30 June Paderewski died today. I was very sorry.

1 July Many tributes are being paid on the wireless to Paderewski. I am listening to Beethoven's Moonlight Sonata being played very beautifully by Iso Ellinson. The sirens have just gone in M/cr (6.30pm) and there is some gun-fire and some planes are about. Petrol has been cut down by a gallon a month and we have to keep a sort of log now showing every gallon used. Finland has declared war on Russia and they are fighting all along the frontier.

3 July Went to town in morning and tried to do some shopping.

Every shop had queues miles long and Mum absolutely refused to queue up as it is really quite unnecessary. Cherries were 5/- per lb and there is not a new potato to be had. Bought 2 pairs of sheer silk stockings for Mum.

8 July We went to the Palace, M/cr to see 'Lady Behave'. It is the first musical comedy of the war and is on here before going to London. Pat Kirkwood, Stanley Lupino, Sally Grey and Mantovani and his Orchestra were in it. It was excellent and very funny.

A south coast town was blitzed last night.

9 July The Americans have taken over Iceland from us for the duration to relieve our men. President Roosevelt said they must go further afield to guard the Western Hemisphere. The Vichy people in Syria have requested an armistice from us.

13 July We have signed a treaty of alliance with Russia.

18 July There is a big battle to save Leningrad. Over 9 million men are in the field and fighting is on a scale bigger than ever before known in history.

25 July We and the Empire and America have ordered the freezing of all Japanese assets. Japan gets 90% of its war materials from us.

3 August Japan is massing two armies and it looks as though she will attack Russia. The war is spreading all over the world and that would bring America in. It looks like being years before the war is over. Last night we raided Berlin, Kiel and Hamburg. Light raids on NE and E.

13 August The Germans are making more headway in Russia now, worst luck. We sent big forces of bombers over last night and lost about 13.

14 August They announced a special speech by Mr Attlee, Lord Privy Seal and Deputy P.M. at 3 o'clock. After all that fuss, it was that Mr Churchill and President Roosevelt have met in mid-Atlantic for talks and have published a joint policy of 8 points.

15 August The P.M. and Roos. met on the Prince of Wales, our newest battleship and were together 3 days. The Germans have encircled Smolensk which has been evacuated and given up. We sent over 300 bombers last night and lost 12.

8 September The Germans have surrounded Leningrad. Last night our bombers made the heaviest raid ever on Berlin and we lost 22 bombers.

9 September We went to the Celebrity Concert at the Champness Hall. Norman Allin, Isobel Baillie and Walter Widdop sang, while Graham Adams and Albert Kinsey entertained. It was simply lovely and Norman Allin sang very well.

We have landed Canadian and British troops on the islands of Spitzbergen – have evacuated all the miners and their families and desolated the land. good work! The Germans have been thwarted!

Yesterday we lost 2 Flying Fortresses.

21 September The Russians say that their troops have evacuated Kiev. Listened to Lord Haw-Haw reading the English news from Germany. He does talk some drivel.

23 September The Great Day! [started at RMCM] Got to the College and had to hang about all morning fixing up lessons.

9 October The Germans are within 120 miles of Moscow and there is bitter fighting.

13 October Last night there was a terrific raid over here. I slept through it all. 3 bombs fell on Norden and lots of shells at Littleborough. Poor Gran was petrified. The night fighters were up too and they say the noise was terrific. We are an interception area now. Damage done in Bolton.

20 October The Huns are within 60-80 miles of Moscow and a state of siege has been declared there. They are going to defend the city to the last man and the last inch. The situation is grave.

21 October Over 50 Frenchmen have been shot as reprisals for the shooting of a German officer.

29 October The greengrocer made a very great concession and gave me a lb. of oranges meant only for children under 6 – was I bucked! The first we have had since soon after the beginning of war.

PROGRAMME

PART I.

1.—GRAHAM ADAMS will entertain.

2. SONG.—"The Vulcan's Song" (Philemon et Baucis)........*Gounod*

NORMAN ALLIN.

3. ARIAS.

(*a*) "You who have knowledge" (Voi che sapete).
(*b*) "I forget what I am" (Non so pui) from Figaro..........*Mozart*

ISOBEL BAILLIE.

4. VIOLIN SOLOS.

Concerto in E minor (2nd and 3rd movements) ....*Mendelssohn*

JOAN SPENCER.

5. SONGS.—(*a*) "On wings of Song" ....*Mendelssohn*
(*b*) "Impatience" ....*Schubert*

WALTER WIDDOP.

6. DUET.—"Give me thy hand, O fairest" Don Giovanni ......*Mozart*

ISOBEL BAILLIE, NORMAN ALLIN.

7. HUMOROUS SELECTION.—ALBERT KINSEY.

INTERVAL 5 mins.

Part of the programme of the Celebrity Concert on 9 September

L - ROCHDALE

4th, 1941, at 7 p.m.

MUSICAL CULTURE LIMITED

presents

THE LONDON PHILHARMONIC ORCHESTRA

(*Leader* - REGINALD MORLEY)

Conductor :

LESLIE HEWARD

Programme and Notes, price 6d.

The London Philharmonic in the Champness Hall, 4 November

31 October An American destroyer has been sunk by a U-boat off Iceland – much anger in USA. We bombed Naples and Benghazi again and made offensive sweeps over Germany and France. Lost 6 planes.

1 November Heavy fighting around Tula and the Germans claim to have penetrated the outer defences and be fighting in the suburbs. They are throwing troops into the fight to get through the Crimea.

2 November A German bishop has preached against the Nazis and said that it is the cruelty of the Gestapo that will be the cause of their fall.

7 November Collected our new pink ration books for tinned foods. Stalin has made a speech on the anniversary of their revolution. Rather too much propaganda.

14 November Dreadful news! The aircraft-carrier Ark Royal has been sunk – after the Germans claimed it for years now. She was sunk by planes whilst in tow. All men from the Ark Royal are safe except 18 and they might be on ships which have not already reported to base.

15 November There is now only 1 missing from the Ark Royal – isn't it wonderful.

20 November Marvellous news! We have started an offensive in Libya. For the first time we meet the Huns equally well armed. Owing to the surprise we have got 50 miles since Tuesday. They say that it will be won or lost quickly and will be most decisive and important to the whole course of the war.

23 November We have captured Bardia and our men in Tobruk have fought their way out. The enemy have lost half their total complement of tanks, and though our losses are heavy they are considerably less. The Germans are trying to rush aircraft over from the other side of the Med. – our air supremacy was established the first day.

The Germans claim to have captured Rostov-on-Don.

25 November Pouishnoff played a programme of Chopin exquisitely – I was spellbound all the way through [recital at Champness Hall].

28 November Things are going favourably in Libya. We have advanced further west. Over 40 enemy ships have been hit in Med. during past month. Russians have counter-attacked strongly in several sectors. Gondar, the last Italian stronghold in Abyssinia, has surrendered. Whoopee!! Conversation still going on between USA and Japan.

30 November The Russians have counter-attacked and have recaptured Rostov. In Libya we have reached the coast S. of Benghazi – as far as we got before. A German General commanding a Panzer division has been captured. Rommel's forces are completely surrounded.

1 December Mum and I went to town to do some shopping and our net result was one basket of cress – were we fed up!

2 December No news from Libya since German counter-attack. HMAS Sydney has been sunk by U-boats. There are no survivors as yet. It is such a tragedy.

3 December Still no news from Libya – sounds rather ominous.

5 December Mum and I unravelled one of Dad's pullovers to make him a pair of socks – these 'ere are 'ard times!!

At last news! Heavy fighting has started again in Libya after a lull for refitting.

7 December JAPAN ATTACKS AMERICA. Sensational news. Today Japan launched attacks on Thailand, Malaya and various Pacific islands including Pearl Harbour, the US naval base, where quite a lot of damage was done.

8 December US is at war with Axis and we have declared war on Japan. Thailand has agreed to transit of Japs. through their country. Menace to Singapore. Hong Kong is being invaded by land. Parliament hurriedly called. Heard speech by Mr. Churchill.

9 December Jap. landings on Guam and near Manila and several other islands. Heavy fighting in Malay Pa. Americans have suffered heavy losses and they admit to having been caught napping.

10 December The battleships Prince of Wales and Repulse – our two newest ships – have been sunk. We have held up the offensive on Hong Kong. Still engagements in Pacific islands. Russians are advancing in most sectors – hurray. In Libya we have relieved Tobruk. Only 3 sectors of organised Axis resistance there.

16 December Some good news from Russia and Libya. Pacific not so good.

19 December We have evacuated Penang, off coast of Malaya. Jap. troops have attempted landing on Hong Kong. Rather bad news. We have started bombing the Scharnhorst, Gneisenau and Prinz Eugen at Brest once more.

21 December Hitler has taken over Supreme Command of the German army!!!

31 December Reviewing the war situation, things are going excellently in Russia, Libya and the Atlantic Life Line – the only dark spot is the loss of Hong Kong and the threat to the Philippines and Singapore. However, I am sure we shall never let Singapore go if it is humanly possible to hold it, and once the Americans get going, the Japs. don't stand a chance. We enter 1942 in a far brighter position than we did 1941, even if Mr. C. does talk about our preparations for 1944 and 1945!

I am convinced things will come right soon.

Act I, Scene 3

The Royal Manchester College of Music

AFTER PASSING THE INTERMEDIATE HIGHER exams in the summer of 1941 when I was sixteen, I decided that I wanted to study singing at the Royal Manchester College of Music. My parents were fully supportive and my grandfather contacted an old friend of his youth, the famous bass singer Norman Allin, who had made a national name in oratorio and opera. He was a professor at the RMCM and, after I was accepted, agreed to become my teacher. The audition was not a particularly arduous affair and consisted of singing one song – Edward MacDowell's *To a Wild Rose* – and playing a short piano piece. I was interviewed by the principal, R J Forbes, a rather small but forbidding, unsmiling man, who had been accompanist to a celebrated diva – Tetrazzini – on a world tour. From the start I found him an unsympathetic character, sardonic and totally lacking in charm and charisma. He was, though, a fine musician and ran the College very successfully indeed. I think they must have been short of students and thankful for any who would pay the very modest fees of the day. There was I, never having had a singing lesson in my life, accepted on a double diploma course to study for the ARMCM, Performers and Teachers, starting in September 1941.

I was, as promised, allocated to Norman Allin for singing lessons, to Annie Lord for piano second study, and went to Maria Valgimigli for Italian and Mrs. Leslie Langford for German. James Dawber was the harmony teacher, R.J. took the opera class, and the great James Bernard, who had been Robert Donat's teacher, the drama class. During the previous years I had been to a number of orchestral concerts and solo instrumental recitals at Rochdale's Champness Hall, but had heard relatively little singing. I was therefore like a sponge soaking up every possible opportunity to learn new repertoire and to experience every type of music I could possible hear and learn. The Hallé Orchestra was busy giving concerts at the old Free Trade Hall and used to tour the northern towns, coming occasionally to Rochdale. So did the Liverpool Philharmonic Orchestra, and we used to listen avidly to violinists such as Henry Holst – who also taught violin at the RMCM –, Thomas Matthews, Jean

Pougnet, cellist Pierre Fournier and a host of others. I became very friendly with a violin student at College who was a Jewish refugee from Germany. He had hardly a penny to his name and used to do fire-watching at night to earn a few bob. This meant spending the hours of darkness outside on a roof or top floor of vulnerable buildings on guard against incendiary bombs, armed with a stirrup-pump and buckets of water and sand – the standard high-tech equipment of the day. He was the most passionately dedicated person I had ever met and carried his enthusiasm into his personal life too. He used to telephone me at home and play long stretches of a sonata or concerto, raving about its harmonies and beauties of expression. My father thought it all very peculiar and would get quite exasperated when I monopolised – as he called it – the phone for an hour at a time. When Yehudi Menuhin came over from America on tour, we would travel over to Liverpool in great discomfort on a slow, dirty, train, to hear him play at the new Philharmonic Hall with the LPO – not yet Royal – and I cannot hear the Mendelssohn violin concerto even today without being transported back to those wartime revelations.

It was a tragedy for me when, after just over a year of study with Norman Allin, he decided he could no longer continue to make the journey up to Manchester from his home in London and resigned from the College. He had been a perfect first teacher for me. He was careful with such a young voice, never allowing me to oversing, and tried to give only appropriate repertoire. Of course, like all young singers one aspired to the great operatic arias and would warble, for pleasure, *Mi chiamano Mimi* and insisting, in opera class, on trying my hand with the *Ave Maria* and *Salce* from Otello. I was then a soprano, the young voice being nowhere near maturity. For this reason it was a disaster when Lillian Stiles-Allen replaced Norman Allin. She was a short, completely round woman, as broad as she was tall, with a fine dramatic soprano and a great name as an opera singer. She declared that I was a coloratura soprano and had me singing up to F in alt with a pencil between my teeth. She may have had success with other students but for me it almost brought my budding career to an abrupt close. I must have been tougher though because I ended my three years study in July 1944 with both diplomas successfully gained, and enough voice to perform Granados' *La Maja y el Ruiseñor* at the student concert on 13 June.

During the three years there I had made some lasting friendships, some of whom I still meet today. Joan Spencer, the violinist, was a pupil of Henry Holst and a fine, natural player who was something of a young prodigy. She played the Max Bruch violin concerto at a Prom quite soon after leaving

ROYAL MANCHESTER COLLEGE OF MUSIC

Students' Concert

TUESDAY, 13th JUNE, 1944, at 7-0 p.m.

PROGRAMME

ORGAN ....Praeludium from Sonata in F major.......... *W. H. Dayas*
ALBERT KNOWLES (MR. DAWBER)

RECIT. & ARIA......" Gold now is common "
" How green our fertile pastures " (Solomon).... *Handel*
ELLEN READ (MISS THURSTON)

OBOE.........Siciliana and Vivace from Concerto Grosso in B flat........ *Handel*
BERNARD O'KEEFE (MRS. BARBIROLLI)

ARIA..............The Maja and the Nightingale (Goyescas).......... *Granados*
PAMELA BOWDEN (MISS STILES-ALLEN)

PIANO...............Concerto in C (1st movement)................ *Beethoven*
DOROTHY ROWLEY (MISS PIERCE)

SONGS ....Die junge Nonne
Auf dem Wasser zu singen .... *Schubert*
PATRICIA COXON (MISS STILES-ALLEN)

FLUTE ....Sonata in G, No. 3...................... *Handel*
MARY HODGSON (MR. LINGARD)

SONGS....................(*a*) Stille Sicherheit .... *Franz*
(*b*) Marienlied .... *Marx*
MARGARET POLLARD (MISS THURSTON)

PIANO ....Italian Concerto........................ *Bach*
ELSIE BROOMHEAD (MISS PIERCE)

ARIA ...." Adieu Forêts " (Jeanne d'Arc) .... *Tchaikovski*
MARY ELLSON (MISS STILES-ALLEN)

VIOLIN .... (*a*) Romance in F...................... *Beethoven*
(*b*) Variation on a theme by Corelli .... *Tartini*
ELIZABETH BOËNDERS (MR. HOLST) *arr. Kreisler*

Accompanists: FLORA KENT, ALBERT HARDIE.

College, and made a successful start to her career as a soloist. Joan later devoted her life to teaching at the Guildhall School of Music and Drama. Marjorie Thomas was a little ahead of me and was studying both singing and piano at the RMCM and taking her Mus B degree at the University at the same time, studying singing with Elsie Thurston and her degree work with H Procter Gregg. She was a star student and I admired her greatly. She was blessed with the same beautiful contralto voice as a student as she was later to use to such effect in her very successful career. Winifred Busfield had a fine, dark dramatic mezzo voice. She decided to return to Scotland where she made a reputation as an outstanding teacher, working both privately and at the Royal Scottish Academy of Music and Drama in Glasgow during a long career. Minnie Bower and Margaret Burton went on to become successful singers, but both died comparatively young. Marion Lowe, a close friend, joined Sadlers Wells Opera and sang leading roles for many years. Richard Lewis had already left by the time I arrived but his name was often mentioned. We later became good friends and colleagues until his death.

Perhaps the most significant friendship started when I met Flora Kent, who was the college's official accompanist. She was kindly, warm and enormously helpful to me, as she was to all the students, and she was to play a great part in my future career. Flora had been a pupil of RJ Forbes and she also found him difficult to deal with, but worse still, although she had a fine, natural talent, she always blamed him for not having provided her with a more secure technique. She played very well indeed but she felt she had to work very hard in order to achieve sufficient facility at the keyboard. A more virtuoso technique would have reduced the stress and anxiety she always felt when playing in public.

It was in July 1944 that I graduated and gained both Teachers' and Performers' ARMCM diplomas. The examiner was Henry Cummings, the distinguished baritone, who said nice things about my performance, and our diplomas were presented, on Graduation Day, by the Hallé's chief conductor, John Barbirolli. I was fascinated by the appearance of this dapper little man who wore matching red and white spotted socks, tie and handkerchief! What a superficial memory to have of him and of that important day! He was already married to the oboist Evelyn Rothwell, who has become a dear and much admired friend, and who, as Lady Barbirolli, has played such a distinguished role in the musical world ever since.

Act I, Scene 4
The Wrens

OUR FAMILY GRADUALLY CAME TO FEEL the impact of the war in the call-up to the forces of the younger generation. My cousin Yvonne had joined the ATS, Roger had joined the Navy as an engineer Midshipman, Uncle Jimmy, Marjorie's husband, had left his bespoke tailoring business and joined the RAF where he was drafted to a barrage-balloon unit. Not the most glamorous of postings but *someone* had to discourage the bombers from flying low over their targets. Having escaped call-up at age seventeen through being a student, I became liable for service after graduation. Wanting some degree of choice about where I should go, I volunteered for the WRNS (Women's Royal Naval Service) – this being the most prestigious and apparently agreeable of the women's services. I was duly sent for medical examination and interview and told that the only vacancies available were as cooks and stewards or as radio mechanics. Faced with such a choice, and being told I would be eligible to train as a radio mechanic since I had credits in maths and physics, I took that option, not without some misgivings.

In due course my call-up papers came through and on 30 August 1944 I left home for the first time, having been ordered to present myself at a place called Tulliechuan Castle, Balloch, Scotland. This turned out to be on the shores of Loch Lomond. I met some other girls on the train who were also joining up. We arrived at this grim-looking smallish stone castle in the grounds of which were a number of Nissen huts. We were directed there to find our sleeping accommodation. It was quite exciting but at the same time a huge shock to find oneself sleeping on a two-tier bunk in an enormous hut with some thirty or so other girls, with only a small cupboard to stow one's belongings and toilet facilities that were, at best, basic and communal.

From the very first day, and I don't quite remember how it happened, six of us formed a group. We must somehow have realised immediately that we had something in common, but the extraordinary thing is that we not only stuck together throughout those six weeks of basic training but stayed together throughout our nine months of rigorous schooling to become radio-mechanics;

kept in touch when we were scattered to different naval bases or air stations, and have remained friends for the rest of our lives. There was Anne Margaret Donaldson (Maggie D), a Scot from West Kilbride, of whom more later. Margaret Bennett (Maggie B) was a serious, studious girl, the most reserved of us all. She married and had three children, living just outside Salisbury. The liveliest and most amusing of us was Pam Chasteney who came from Purley in Surrey. She had an infectious sense of humour, and especially of the ridiculous, and was always having dramatic things happen to her – like the time she caught headlice on the train to Glasgow and the whole camp got involved in ridding her hair of the unwanted guests. Pam later married a distinguished physician who became one of the Queen's doctors. Pat Christie was a delightful, high-spirited girl who married and had two children, living in Cheshire and having a happy, settled existence. Lastly, there was Joy Alexander, the tomboy and trouble-magnet. She was a tiny bundle of energy, always willing to embark on some prank or other, and constantly attracting the wrath of the NCOs and officers. It was as much as she could do to appear neatly dressed in uniform – always a button was off or shoes unshined, and one of my joyful memories is of her appearing late on parade with her round cap stuck onto the side of her head and the petty officer yelling 'Alexander! Yer 'at should be at fifteen degrees, not for'y five'.

We were not given our uniforms immediately as we were on a fortnight's probation. The WRNS was not actually, at that time, one of the armed forces and was not under Kings' Regulations. We were regarded as volunteers and it was actually possible for us, at any time during our service, to leave and get out without becoming deserters. All Wrens stayed in the service because they wanted to and not because they had to. Consequently the first two weeks were made as tough as they could possible be in order to weed out those who couldn't stay the course. Instead of uniforms we were given what we nicknamed 'Bloody bluettes' – a sort of overall-type dress in coarse blue material with a fabric belt on which was a small purse. We must have been given the round sailor hats, I suppose, as we had to learn the proper naval salute. Part of the initial training was to teach us to refer to everything in naval terms. Our camp was the ship, our beds were bunks, the walls were bulkheads, the lavatories were the heads, and so on.

The part I liked was the parades and the drills. Somehow, learning to march and to carry out all the movements of the drills satisfied my feeling for the rhythm and unison of the marching, and I threw myself into it with gusto. The downside was the food, and our constant ravenous hunger. We would grab slices of bread and lash masses of margarine and brown sugar on to them as a start to meals. We couldn't wait to be served with the basic stews and mash, with suet puddings and thick yellow custard for dessert. Nearby in the village was a little café where we would dash at every free moment. There we were offered a choice of Spam and chips, sausage and chips or egg and chips – always chips. We gobbled them up with relish, heavily laced with tomato ketchup or HP sauce.

One day, we had a free afternoon and the six of us decided to walk along by the loch. It was a fine, sunny autumn day and we spotted a rather grand house away in the distance. Fairly soon, a Land Rover driven by a nice-looking man stopped and asked if we'd like a lift. We accepted with alacrity and piled in. As usual, Pam C (known as that to distinguish her from Pam B, myself) chattered away to the driver and said 'How awesome that big house up there is – wonder if it belongs to some frightfully rich laird.' She was covered with embarrassment to discover that 'Actually, it's my home', from our kind driver. It took Pam a long time to live that down.

Eventually we were deemed worthy of the uniform, duly sworn-in and became fully-fledged Ordinary Wrens. At the end of six weeks, we were given travel warrants, and our group despatched by train to London. Oh glory! Civilisation again. We were to be quartered at New College in Finchley Road – a large red-brick building which was a haven of comfort after our privations in Scotland. It had been a theological college and the décor was elegant, with lovely oak panelling, comfortable rooms with easy chairs, a large garden and, best of all, smaller cabins. We dashed around and pounced on a six-bunk room on the top floor which we annexed for ourselves. We disposed ourselves on the three two-tier bunks and quickly made ourselves at home.

The room is still very clear in my memory – and one incident in particular stands out. When we arrived in London in late 1944, the buzz-bombs, or doodle bugs, were just about starting to arrive. These were small automatic planes filled with high-explosive. They would fly over southern England to London, if not shot down on the way, and then, at some point the engine would cut out and the bomb would drop. As we could hear them coming, we had some warning and when they droned on overhead and away, sighs of relief all round. When the engine stopped, however, you knew it would fall somewhere nearby and you'd dive for cover. We had quite a number of these experiences but the one that sticks in my mind was being awakened one night to an almighty shout 'Look out, there's one coming' and sitting up in my top bunk to see the door flung wide open and Joy sprawling and sliding on her front over the polished floor. The bomb did land but only near enough to shake the house, and we were convulsed by the unorthodox air-raid warning.

Every day we would be ferried by coach to Walthamstow Technical College where we were given our basic grounding in electrics and radio theory and maintenance. It was hard going – at the end of every week there was a test and monthly a more serious exam. If you failed any one of them you could not go on with the course. We had a long-suffering instructor for our group called Mr Sutton who somehow managed to keep our disparate lot in order and keep us interested in the subject. At the end of the 20 week course we sang to him our version of the music hall song *Oh Mister Porter*. It ran:

Oh Mister Sutton, what shall we do,
They're sending us to Petersfield and we want to stay with you.
Bring us back to London as quickly as you can.
Oh Mister Sutton, you darling little man.

He was obviously embarrassed but also pleased – but he couldn't bring us back to London and that was the last most of us ever saw of him. Except – one day many years later I had a letter from him. He had been to a concert to hear me sing and had remembered the trainee Wren after all that time.

While we were in London we made the most of its attractions and were off to the West End on every free day. We would go to the Salad Bowl at Lyons' Corner House where you could eat as much as you wanted for a set sum – probably about half a crown (two shillings and sixpence or twelve and a half pence today). The salads were delicious and we went back again and again for refills. We sometimes went to the Services Clubs where there were dances and one could meet soldiers, sailors and airmen. We were a bit afraid of the Americans – over-paid, over-sexed and over here, as the saying went. We were, on the whole, very innocent! Very grandly we occasionally patronised the bars of the Berkeley and the Ritz and considered ourselves the ultimate in sophistication. We were saddened to have to leave New College just before Christmas and move to Highgate, to Channing School, which had been requisitioned by the Navy for the duration. It was nothing like as elegant or as comfortable, but we had to put up with it.

My sharpest memory of that time was of putting on a Christmas concert with the help of Maggie D, who had a pretty soprano voice. We slogged our way through the winter months with the daily coach runs to Walthamstow in the dark both morning and evening, and most evenings after supper were spent in doing homework or swotting for tests and exams. At last we endured the

Saturday 21 July at 7

GOD SAVE THE KING

Conductor: Basil Cameron

Overture, Cockaigne (In London Town)	*Elgar*
Rhapsody on a Theme of Paganini for Pianoforte and Orchestra	*Rachmaninoff*

Conductor: Sir Adrian Boult

Prelude, The Forgotten Rite	*John Ireland*
Symphony No. 5, in C minor	*Beethoven*

Conductor: Basil Cameron

Organ Concerto in D minor (Op. 7, No. 4)	*Handel—Wood*

Conductor: Sir Adrian Boult

Aria, Ritorna vincitor (Aïda)	*Verdi*
(a) Memorial Fanfare (b) March, Crown Imperial	*William Walton*

STILES-ALLEN

Solo Pianoforte MOISEIWITSCH

Solo Organ MARCEL DUPRÉ

The Prom prospectus for July-September 1945 – (below) the opening concert, one of many attended while serving in the Wrens in London

final exams and news of our next postings. When the results were announced, all six of us had passed – but we were shattered to hear that the top two in the class would be retained as instructors to the next intake at Walthamstow.

Shattered because top marks went to Maggie B, third to a girl called Rita Brown, and second to myself. Maggie B. threw a most uncharacteristic tantrum and stormed off to the CO's office to protest loudly. Amazingly she somehow persuaded them to let her go to a station, and this left Rita and myself to stay behind.

However, before this could happen, we were all going to be sent to a training 'ship' HMS Signal School at Leydene, near Petersfield (referred to in Mr Sutton's ditty), for our final practical training. Off we went in the early spring to find ourselves quartered in a country house, Soberton Towers, shared by a group of ratings who were training as telegraphists in Japanese: one side of the house was for them and the other, severely cordoned off, for us Wrens. Our practical training took place every day in the nearby naval station where first we had morning parade and the flag was raised. Then we dispersed to various huts housing the most enormous ships' transmitters and receivers – we decided the maintenance of these was rather like plumbing. While we were living at Soberton Towers, peace was declared and we celebrated the end of hostilities in Europe with VE Day in June. We had also earlier celebrated my 20th birthday with a party on the lawn and a huge chocolate cake sent by my mother. Heaven knows how she managed it on the rations.

I fell madly in love with one of the telegraphists, a handsome dark-haired lad from Croydon called Steve, who was equally enamoured. Sadly we were soon separated and could not keep in touch, so I never knew what became of him – I hope he survived those awful battles in Japanese waters.

Inevitably this delightful interlude came to an end and finally the six were separated, each of the others going off to a different posting, and myself back to London. This time we were quartered in Chelsea – even further from Walthamstow – and again in a huge, elegant house, in Cheyne Walk on Chelsea Embankment.

We resumed the usual days at the Technical College, but this time with a mixed group of Wrens and ratings. I can't remember anything about our duties, but Rita and I were rather grand now as Leading Wrens, with a chevron added to our sleeves. Promotion was automatic on the completion of the course.

At last came the end of this duty and Rita and I were given postings – mine, horror of horrors, was to a naval base way up in Scotland, fifty miles north of Aberdeen, between Fraserburgh and Peterhead, on land jutting out into the North Sea called Rattray Head. I made my way there with heavy heart, leaving my beloved southern climes for the bitterly cold, stormy, gale-ridden east coast, and my worst fears were realised. It was horrible – and the first thing I did was catch a beastly cold from damp sheets. The job was maintaining the transmitter/receivers on the MTBs – motor torpedo boats – at the base, a task that was viewed with gloomy depression, only relieved by the presence of a personable young sub-lieutenant. Relief came after only four weeks in the form of yet another posting, this time – guess what – to yet another training course. I was required to present myself to HMS Ariel at Runcorn, Lancashire, for the purpose of conversion to aircraft radio and subsequent posting to the Fleet Air Arm. A great bonus was to meet again some old friends from London, among whom was Pam C.

Once again the surroundings were dreary but the course more interesting, with equipment of manageable size and a farewell to condensers and resistances big enough to line a room. During the course, I devised a gadget to fit into a handset to allow the user to cut out unwanted reception while transmitting. I believe this was taken up by the RN but I didn't get any credit for it!

One good thing about this brief period was the proximity to my home which was only about 30 miles distant. I was able to get to Rochdale to see my parents and celebrate my 21st birthday at home.

Instructing ratings at Walthamstow Technical College

Puzzle – find the Wren. RNAS Culham

The course came to an end and I got my final posting. This time I was sent south again, to HMS Hornbill, a Royal Naval Air Station at Culham, near Abingdon. There was a ferry pool of pilots whose task it was to ferry new air-craft from factories for us to fit with transceivers and then to ferry them onward to operational stations. The aircraft we worked on were mostly Seafires, Fireflies and Mosquitos. There was much to enjoy – firstly I got my promotion to Petty Officer Wren and acquired my 'buttons'. This meant gilt uniform buttons instead of black bone ones, and best of all, the tricorne hat instead of the round flat ratings cap. Secondly, I got my own single 'cabin' – privacy at last. Thirdly, the countryside was lovely and we were near enough to be able to go in to Oxford at off-duty times. The local pub was a charming country inn where we popped in for the odd half of local cider.

Among my friends there was another radio mechanic called Barbara whose family lived not far from mine. She had a lovely little MG roadster and we drove up to Lancashire on leave once or twice. Another colleague was a society girl with friends in high places who invited me to visit some undergraduate chums at New College, Oxford. Among them was Anthony Wedgwood-Benn – only later did I realise who he was. Another chum, Alethea, a fair-haired aristocratic girl, fell in love with and later married our CO – an RN Commander.

I was in charge of one of the radio workshops and naturally got to know many of the ferry pilots, who were mostly a good-natured, gregarious lot. One Sunday I was on call and received a message to grab a parachute and report to the squadron for a test flight. I was horrified to discover that the plane we were to test was a Firefly that had been dubbed a rogue, meaning that it had some control fault that couldn't be identified and put right. Added to this, I was ordered to test the radar set in flight, which put me in a quandary as I was trained for radio but not radar. The pilot told me to 'just switch the thing on and see if you get a picture'. All well and good but when we were finally several thousand feet up and my heart in my mouth wondering what nasty surprises the plane might have in store, I couldn't see a thing on the radar screen. We finally landed safely after a few hairy moments and when I told the radar mech. what had happened, he asked 'You did put the shade over the screen to cut out the light, didn't you?' Of course I hadn't.

On the station we had a couple of old Oxford and Anson transport planes which were used to carry spares and other odd jobs and sometimes one could beg a ride – useful on one occasion when I was able to get a lift down to Southampton from where it was easy to go to Bosham, near Chichester, to visit my relatives who were by then living there.

The winter of 1946/47 was one of the most severe in living memory. Snow lay on the ground for ten weeks on end and our existence, living and working in huts on the perimeter of the airfield was one long struggle to keep warm. Before the snow came, I had used some spare time profitably to learn to drive and used to practice on the airfield perimeter track tutored by one of the navy drivers.

It was a considerable relief when my demob papers came through and I finally headed home to Rochdale in late February 1947. Looking back, despite the general mood of desperate live-for-today which gave a kind of glamour to the early years, the overriding impression left by the war years and those immediately following was one of drabness. We gradually became ground down by all the shortages, lack of little luxuries, a constant feeling of deprivation and weariness. Life was undoubtedly hardest for the housewives, struggling to make palatable meals for their families amid surroundings that grew more and more shabby and dull. The blackout was always a trial and the joy in June 1945 when the lights were switched on again was immeasurable. It was perhaps more unbearable that shortages of almost everything lasted into the early 1950s when spirits buoyed up by the adrenalin of war were reduced by the realities of a very hard-won peace. My time in the Wrens was relatively happy and comfortable compared with many who had served overseas and during the darkest war days. But it was with huge relief that I threw off my uniform and bought, as far as the clothing coupons would stretch, some new, pretty and feminine clothes. I shall always remember my first 'New Look' outfit with its calf-length full skirt, jacket with a nipped-in waist and high-heeled court shoes – how we loved Christian Dior!

Act I, Scene 5
More Family Matters

TO DIGRESS FOR A MOMENT, during the war all four of my grandparents died, as also did old Henry Francis and Uncle Leslie, his son. The Francis family had moved before the war from Caberfeigh in Reigate to Copsley, a mansion in the village of Outwood, Surrey. It was a beautiful house, restored and refurbished by them, and had the unheard-of number of seven bathrooms. There was a very large room at one end of the house, used as a family games room, with a full-size billiard table in the centre, at one end a platform on which was an upright piano and a bridge table, and in the middle of one long side was an inglenook fireplace with seats at each side, where a log fire burned in winter. At the other end was an open space where we could dance to the radiogram. The house was furnished with French antique furniture, Louis XVI cabinets, Chinese carpets, huge vases on plinths – and yet it was lived-in and friendly. There was a vast kitchen where Auntie Win would make gorgeous yellow clotted cream on the Aga from milk from her Jersey cow, and daily fresh fruit – peaches, nectarines, strawberries and raspberries in summer – would be brought in, together with the freshest of vegetables. For a time they bred white Samoyed dogs, of which my parents took a puppy back up to Rochdale – it was difficult keeping the long white fur clean in the then much dirtier atmosphere.

It was a house for big family gatherings and we would sit at the long dining table, up to twenty or more people, for my aunt's delicious meals. Always at the head of the table was Grandpa Francis with his larger-than-life personality, the paterfamilias in the Victorian tradition.

By this time the Gubbin grandparents had also moved to nearby Horley where Muriel lived with them in a modest three-bedroom house.

A vivid memory of Copsley is of Uncle Leslie leaning out of his bedroom window potting at grey squirrels, or tree rats as he called them, with a .22 rifle. I don't think he ever hit one.

The Francis family fitted into village life and took part in all the local activities – after all, the games room at Copsley had once been the village hall. On one occasion they were so short of players for the cricket team that even I was drafted in to play and was sent off as long-stop on the edge of the pitch. I don't believe I ever touched the ball but it was a pleasantly lazy afternoon.

Living nearby was a family called Clutterbuck with five children, one of the oldest being Bernard, who fell in love with my cousin Yvonne. When war came he became a lieutenant in the Royal Marines and was captured in Crete in 1942, spending the rest of the war in German prisoner-of-war camps. When he was released in 1945 he came home and after a period of recuperation, he and Yvonne were married at Outwood Parish Church in a double ceremony at which Roger also married a very beautiful girl called Norma. Yvonne was in the ATS and Roger was a Sub-Lieutenant engineer in the RN. Both Bernard and Roger were married in uniform, and I, as the one and only bridesmaid, wore my WRNS uniform.

Bernard and Yvonne later bought a small-holding beside the creek at Bosham, the historic and charming village where King Canute's daughter is buried in the old Saxon church. They had two children, my god-daughter Elizabeth, and son Charles. To complete this saga, after the end of the war and the death of Grandpa Francis, Auntie Win and Uncle Leslie moved to a slightly smaller house in Chislehurst. Their stay there was shortened when Uncle died quite suddenly, leaving Auntie Win bereft. She sold up and built a bungalow on Bosham Creek next to Bernard's nursery. Muriel joined her to live there as both Gubbin grandparents had died within a short time of each other and dear Muriel was left alone. She had had a wartime romance with a Canadian army captain who was married and eventually returned to Canada – another wartime tragedy. During Auntie Win's lifetime she remained the centre, the focus, for the family, with gatherings at Christmas and holiday times, but after her death in the 1970s, we no longer seemed automatically to get together.

Jimmy, the youngest of the cousins, never married and lived with his mother, dying at a comparatively early age in his fifties. Also quite young, Bernard died of cancer. It was thought that the privations he suffered as a prisoner-of-war must have weakened his health and hastened his untimely end.

During the war my parents moved to a stone-built house tucked into a hillside just outside the town and it was there that my beloved mother died of cancer in 1958 and a light went out of my life. My father took an active interest in local government, became a Councillor and then Mayor of Rochdale. He served for some years as a magistrate. He soon remarried a very different lady but one who cared for him well through their retirement to the lovely town of Fowey in Cornwall and then to Wellington in Somerset where he died of a heart attack in 1971. Our dear Fan, as she is affectionately known, returned to Rochdale where she still lives to this day.

Act I, Scene 6
Back to Civvy Street

MY PARENTS GAVE ME A WARM WELCOME on my return from the Wrens, and for weeks I revelled in the comfort and luxury of being cosseted. It took some time to readjust to civilian life and to the freedom of being able to come and go exactly as I liked. I was keen to resume my studies and to get on with my career – but how? After the traumatic change of teachers in the earlier years it was a constant worry that my voice might never recover. I finally decided on a post-graduate year at the RMCM and knew that my best chance of getting the voice back and technique secured was by requesting as my teacher Mrs Leslie Langford. She was a most remarkable lady. As a young singer, she had married the much older Sam Langford who is remembered as one of the greatest music critics of what was then the *Manchester Guardian* (now the *Guardian*). A deeply cultivated man, he also had a passion for cricket and used to write about it for the paper, eventually being followed in these two interests by his successor, Neville Cardus.

The Langford home was a magnet for all the musicians and music lovers of the Manchester area, with many refugees from pre-First World War Germany. They brought with them a wealth of Lieder repertoire, including the songs of Hugo Wolf, then unknown in this country. Leslie Langford flourished in this atmosphere and absorbed the language and the culture with intensity. Her own voice lacked sufficient technique and she was never able to develop her talents, but she did form an intuitive understanding of the voice and an uncanny ability to guide each individual voice in safety – something she had been unable to do for herself. She was an inspired teacher who did some invaluable work with students at the RMCM. When eventually the college and the Northern School of Music were combined to create the Royal Northern College of Music, she continued to teach on the vocal faculty until her retirement, but she never felt that she was truly recognised and felt considerable bitterness towards the administration.

She lived in a turn-of-the century house in Didsbury where she also taught privately and over the years I would visit her and talk singers' talk for hour after hour. She never noticed the time passing as she was totally absorbed in her work, so that lessons could go on and on, with many breaks for cups of tea and discussions. During the years of 1947-9 she painstakingly released and rebuilt my voice, during which it dropped to a deep contralto, then gradually settled into the lighter quality contralto that it was to remain. She was incredibly careful, working slowly to build one note upon the other, always from the middle of the voice outwards. Because of my earlier traumatic experience, she became almost too cautious in exploring the top of the voice.

At the end of the year I was singing quite passably, but with a whole new repertoire to learn of all the contralto roles in oratorio and the song repertoire in lower keys. I rapidly built up a basic list of items, studied the complete oratorios of Bach and Handel, and wondered what to do next.

I can't remember how I heard that Flora Kent, our former official accompanist at the RMCM, who had been such a good friend and support, was looking for someone to share her flat in London following the marriage of her flatmate, the singer Mary Peters. Flora was now working as accompanist to the famous teacher and baritone, Roy Henderson, and Mrs. L said he would be the only one to whom she would entrust me. The next move was obvious. I should ask Flora if I might join her to share her flat and ask Roy Henderson if he would take me on as a pupil.

Yes was the answer from both – and with my parents' blessing, I moved out of the parental home to start my new life in London in September 1949.

Doors open and close for one during life. It is perhaps wise to recognise these openings and go through them, while accepting the closures without battering against them. This was one opening that I knew instinctively was absolutely right and it was indeed the happiest of opportunities.

Act II, Scene 1
To London

MY NEW HOME was on the ground floor of one of the large early Victorian houses in Belsize Park Gardens. Our living room had a bay window below which was a basement area. The house had steps leading up to a portico supported by columns, giving a classical Greek frontage. I loved it and settled happily to share the flat with Flora. She was the ideal companion, kind, generous and always willing to listen to one's problems and to offer sympathy and counsel. She was tremendously popular with all Prof's pupils who endlessly sought her help in coaching them in repertoire, and for her musical insight. For an aspiring singer to have her as a flat-mate was the best possible good fortune and Flora was always ready to discuss the last lesson, what had Prof meant by so-and-so, did she think a breath was better taken here or there, what did the poet really mean on page 2, bar 14, was that top F really better than last week – and so on. The list of Prof's students seems endless but some of those

'Prof' – the baritone Roy Henderson

ARCHWAY CENTRAL HALL
HIGHGATE
Superintendent: Rev. LAWRANCE O. BROOKER

RECITAL
by
Kathleen Ferrier
CONTRALTO
Accompanist: PHYLLIS SPURR
Saturday, 29th April 1950
at 7 p.m.

PROGRAMME · SIXPENCE

who should be mentioned are Norma Procter, Ena Mitchell, Rae Woodland, Derek Hammond-Stroud, John Shirley-Quirk, Joan Stuart, John Cameron, Hervey Alan and many others who are mentioned elsewhere. I hope I'll be forgiven for those I have omitted.

My weekly lessons with Prof were always a challenge. He was happy with Mrs L's preparation of the voice and wanted to continue on the same lines to develop and encourage more brightness and 'ring' into the timbre. He said that the lower voices need to have every bit of 'blade' that they could find in order to be able to carry through an orchestra. He was well-known as Kathleen Ferrier's teacher and at that time she still came occasionally for a lesson – she was my idol and I was thrilled one day when Flora took me around to meet her after a concert. Those who have heard only her recordings have not experienced the joy of her personality and the warmth and generosity of her presence. It was a truly beautiful voice which Prof said had in it a ring of gold. (He told me that mine would have a ring of silver eventually.) It was devastating when we heard of her illness and eventual death, and one of the saddest occasions was her memorial service at which I sang as a member of a BBC group. Actually, hardly a note came out – my throat was completely closed by tears and grief. My mouth made the movements necessary for the words, but of tone there was none. Our conductor, Leslie Woodgate, gave some very odd and suspicious looks in my direction, but I'm afraid there was nothing to be done.

I knew that I was not yet ready to start a serious career and that more time must be spent on technique. My voice was not a big, sturdy instrument but rather soft-grained, so I needed every scrap of support and focus to give it viability. How we worked! Sometimes plunged into deepest despair, sometimes euphoria, I decided to give myself one year, after which time I would have to look for a school teaching job. The very thought filled me with horror but I knew that there had to be a target to aim for. In the event, I just made it.

The first necessity was to find some kind of work to pay the rent. Prof spoke of the value of experiencing some professional chorus singing so I applied to the BBC for a place in their ad hoc chorus. This was a list of professional singers who could be gathered to form various sized groups for broadcasts and public concerts – sometimes to be stiffening for the big,

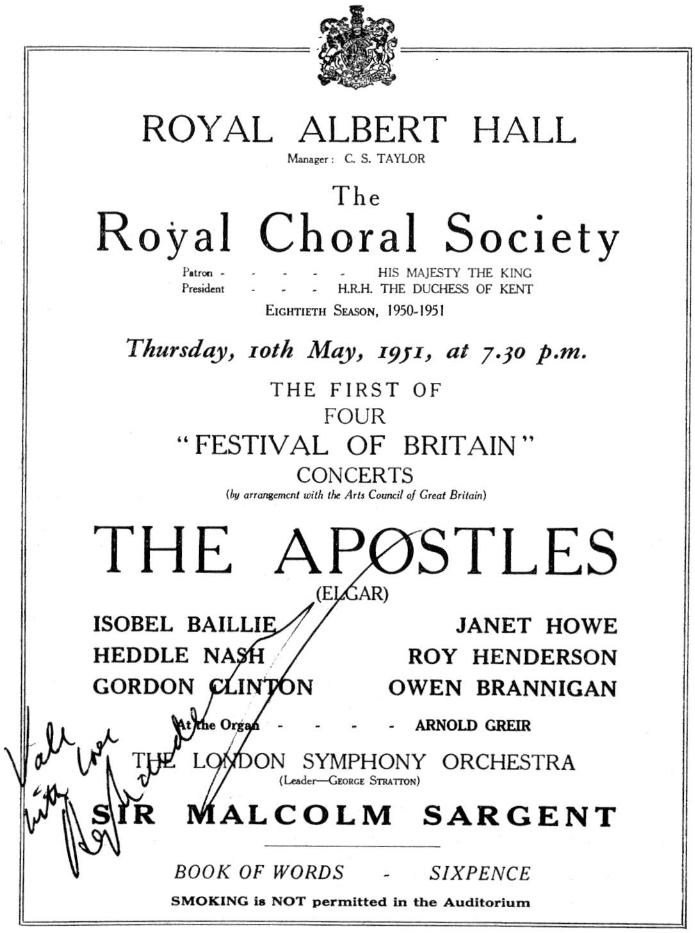
ROYAL ALBERT HALL
Manager: C. S. TAYLOR

The
Royal Choral Society

Patron - HIS MAJESTY THE KING
President - H.R.H. THE DUCHESS OF KENT
EIGHTIETH SEASON, 1950-1951

Thursday, 10th May, 1951, at 7.30 p.m.

THE FIRST OF
FOUR
"FESTIVAL OF BRITAIN"
CONCERTS
(by arrangement with the Arts Council of Great Britain)

THE APOSTLES
(ELGAR)

ISOBEL BAILLIE — JANET HOWE
HEDDLE NASH — ROY HENDERSON
GORDON CLINTON — OWEN BRANNIGAN

At the Organ - ARNOLD GREIR

THE LONDON SYMPHONY ORCHESTRA
(Leader—GEORGE STRATTON)

SIR MALCOLM SARGENT

BOOK OF WORDS - SIXPENCE
SMOKING is NOT permitted in the Auditorium

Prof's retirement performance in 1951

amateur, BBC Choral Society. Members of the ad hoc chorus were freelance, as opposed to the BBC Singers (who formed two groups, the A and B Singers), who were some sixteen in number and under full-time contract. Some of the Singers were quite well-known, in particular a soprano called Marjorie Avis, who was often given solos – a diminutive, highly skilled lady.

The audition was in studio 3E, Broadcasting House, on 17 October 1949 and the request was to bring along two contrasting items. I can't remember what I sang. There was also a stiff sight-singing test. The accompanist on the day was Josephine Lee, one of the BBC stalwarts. All ad hoc singers had to be excellent sight-singers since rehearsal times were limited and teaching the notes was simply not an option. Luckily I was quite a good reader with reasonable relative, though not perfect, pitch. It must have been good enough because a letter came a few days later saying I was accepted, and offering an engagement there and then.

This was the start of a blissful period. I was kept busy right from the first. Usually there would be anything from one to five full days of rehearsals for any given performance. We would often meet in the Waldegrave Hall, a hall in a basement on Duke St, opposite the side of Selfridges. The sessions would be timed from, say, 11.00 to 13.00 and 14.00 to 17.00, and one of the chorus masters would be in charge, either Harold Noble or Cyril Gell, and sometimes even Leslie Woodgate, the principal chorus master.

The recordings would be made in studios in different parts of London – often at the Maida Vale studios for the bigger performances and in front of invited audiences, or from time to time at the Royal Festival Hall or the Royal Albert Hall. I took part many times in Proms at the latter over the next two years. There were many friends among the other singers and we had great fun and camaraderie. From the beginning one of the older sopranos who had been singing with the BBC Scottish Singers for many years, up in Edinburgh during the war, befriended me and took me under her wing. She was Sheenagh McLean, who became one of my dearest friends, together with her husband Rowland Carr, a cellist with the Covent Garden Orchestra, and their son Gordon who later became a gifted BBC producer. Sheenagh was an excellent dressmaker and used to make evening gowns for me, and later on became an indispensable baby-sitter for my little daughter.

The variety of music we performed was immense. The BBC was the greatest promoter of music in the world and was at that time ready to finance expensive, large-cast works which no other bodies could afford. We would sing chamber works requiring small groups of only 20-30, unaccompanied, or take part in massive choral and orchestral works with anything from four to ten soloists. The breadth of repertoire and the many international conductors we worked under made this the most fantastic training ground for a young singer. Among the concerts we did was a weekly programme, *Songs from the Shows*, on Fridays in the Paris Cinema, rehearsing all day for the show at 8 to 8.45pm. By the middle of 1950 my diary shows rehearsals and concerts every day for weeks on end.

During this period of my life work was not solely for the BBC. I was also building up a number of small solo performances, maybe a *Messiah* for Woodford Choral Society or a series of schools concerts for the Arts Council, who would audition musicians and send us to two schools somewhere in the London area – one in the morning and one in the afternoon – short recitals which we had to present to the children and try to involve their attention.

There were some less conventional venues. On one occasion I was booked to give a short recital at Wormwood Scrubs prison. A lot of thought had to be given to the programme to try to please a literally captive audience of unknown tastes. Obviously some popular classics would be acceptable and included were a few well-known operatic arias, among them the *Habañera* from Carmen. I was surprised by the enthusiastic reception and even more so when afterwards one of the men came up and said ''Ere, I know that tune you just sung. It's from that Carmen Jones, innit?'

There were also Masonic dinners at which I would be engaged to sing a group of songs to a smoke-filled room full of men, sometimes with ladies also present on ladies' nights. These would take place in venues such as the Connaught Rooms, the Abercorn Rooms, and the larger hotels. I did not enjoy these very much as the repertoire had to be fairly light classical and popular operatic arias, and the acoustics were usually difficult, 'dead' and unhelpful. But the audiences were appreciative and the money was useful, to say nothing of the experience gained in presenting and communicating the programmes. The man who was most helpful at this time and gave me plenty of work was an organist from Woodford in Essex called Wagstaff – known to his friends as Waggy. He gave me concerts at his church, St John's, Buckhurst Hill, and neighbouring ones, as well as the dinners, and his kindness and help are never to be forgotten. On Good Friday, 7 April 1950 I sang the solos in Messiah for a fee of 2 guineas! A Masonic dinner in September paid 3 guineas and I sang *O Peaceful England, Love could I only tell thee, Dream O'Day Jill* and *I know where I'm goin'*. Other dinner programmes would include *Softly awakes my heart*, *Seguidilla* from *Carmen, A Birthday* by Cowen, *These you have loved* – and other ballads.

Amongst the ad hoc chorus was a singer called John McCarthy who was a 'fixer', which meant that he put together groups of freelance singers for other promoters. He quickly started to offer me work and so I became a member of several other professional choruses, the Ambrosian Singers, the Geraint Jones Singers, and other perhaps nameless groups but mostly composed of the same individuals, depending on availability. Sometimes there were solo lines to be allocated and more and more often the contralto or mezzo ones would be given to me.

It was remarkable that at one time the alto line of the Ambrosian Singers consisted of Jean Allister, Heather Harper (before she became a soprano), Helen Watts and myself – all to go on to make solo careers.

Occasionally we would be asked to go out of London – once to an Eisteddfod involving a very long coach ride to Wales, a concert in the pouring rain in an iron-roofed hall where nothing could be heard for the pounding of the torrent on the roof, and a long, dreary ride back home. Much better was a trip to Paris in 1951 with Professor (later Sir) Anthony Lewis to record Blow's *Venus and Adonis* for the newly-established label L'Oiseau Lyre. In the cast were Margaret Ritchie as Venus; Gordon Clinton as Adonis; Margaret Field-Hyde as Cupid; and a chorus of eight.

It was autumn and Paris was magical – we were invited to a final dinner at a restaurant near the Eiffel Tower by Mrs Dyer, the owner of the company, who presented each of us with a watercolour by the famous artist Marie Laurencin and a little book about John Blow. I ate oysters for the first time and had horrendous indigestion.

A second Paris trip to record the Monteverdi Vespers was memorable for Heather Harper getting stuck in the hotel's tiny wrought-iron lift where we could see her suspended between floors. Tony Lewis was a genial conductor and the recordings were swiftly and competently completed.

Another experience was to take part in the sound tracks of films out at Shepperton and Denham Studios – the details escape me but I do recall Monica Sinclair, the mezzo, singing both tracks of the duet, the *Barcarolle* from *Tales of Hoffmann*. The music we sang was not all serious, by any means. Once I was a backing singer for the popular vocalist Anne Shelton, and when working with the Peter Knight Singers one could be faced with anything. In a jazz ensemble he used to walk along the line, stop in front of one and say 'Less vib, dear' – after one had worked endlessly to find the right kind of vibrato!

For a while, the BBC booked me as one of The Eight Voices. This was a group which did a weekly spot in a variety programme conducted by Ray Jenkins, a Welsh light music director. We would gather in the studio at 9 am and be presented with scraps of manuscript bearing our single lines of music. Since it was often in eight-part harmony, we were each alone in a part, and given no idea what the others were singing. There were several numbers to be rehearsed and by 11 am we would join the orchestra to continue rehearsal. The broadcast would take place at 1 pm and last half an hour. One particular day stands out as one of the artists in the programme was the young Peter Sellars, and we had a great chance to watch him at close quarters.

Other variety-type programmes used to be recorded at the old Camden Theatre with the BBC Concert Orchestra and Stanford Robinson. Once we sang in Delius's incidental music to *Hassan* – the play was performed by members of the BBC Repertory Company and the female lead character was played by Marjorie Westbury, that most versatile and appealing of radio actresses. I remember the spine-chilling effect of the young lovers' walk to execution.

On a much lighter occasion there, a variety programme featured George Robey, already an old man. He was a brilliant cartoonist and he made a sketch of himself in seconds which he gave to me and which I have to this day.

There were occasional forays into television, quite often in the popular light music programme conducted by Eric Robinson, younger brother of Stanford Robinson. It was entitled *Music for You.* We were used as a small choral group singing medleys of favourite songs, with occasionally a solo spot for one of us. I caused family mirth among my cousins by appearing dressed in Welsh national costume complete with stovepipe hat singing a folk song. Another time I became Scottish, singing *My ain folk.* Much later, in 1954, Eric booked me as a guest star on one of the same series.

Self-portrait sketched by George Robey during broadcast rehearsal at the Camden Theatre

Act II, Scene 2
Glyndebourne Chorus

BY THE AUTUMN OF 1950 Prof and I decided it was time to try for the Glyndebourne Chorus. It was well known that many future soloists received early experience at Glyndebourne and Prof himself had sung leading roles there since its first season in 1936. I duly applied for an audition and was accepted. I was to take part in a new production, Mozart's *Idomeneo*.

Prior to this, the only time I had taken part in an opera was to be one of a tiny chorus of four in Donizetti's one-act opera *Il Campanello di Notte* or *The Night Bell*, given a week's run at the Fortune Theatre, and another week up in Chester. The soprano in the small group was Stella Quilley, wife of Denis Quilley, the actor/singer who used to come to the theatre to meet Stella and who became a good friend. He was later to star in many a musical, including the name part in Sondheim's *Sweeney Todd* and in a hilarious *La Cage aux Folles*. The impresario for this venture was one Ernst Urbach and among the cast were Ian Wallace, Bruce Boyce and Bruna Maclean.

So by the time I went to Glyndebourne in May 1951 I had virtually no experience of acting and stage work – but what better way to learn than with the inspiring and charismatic director Carl Ebert. His work with the chorus was incredibly detailed and he gave each one of us an individual character to develop. He was also a very handsome man with a mane of white hair and bags of charm – of course we were all in love with him.

The conductor was Fritz Busch who, with Ebert, had formed the leading team at Glyndebourne for several years. Sparks flew when musical and dramatic interests conflicted but overall they were a superbly successful combination. Sadly, did we but know, it was to be Busch's last season as he was to die suddenly later in the year. I was fortunate indeed to be there that year.

The protagonist in *Idomeneo* was Richard Lewis, who gave a series of magnificent performances, singing with authority and rich warm tone. On one occasion, he was standing on a small hill with us chorus members ranged in tiers below, imploring him to spare his daughter Ilia. I happened to be on the

THE GLYNDEBOURNE OPERA

In the original Italian

IDOMENEO

Re Di Creta

OSSIA

ILIA ED IDAMANTE

Dramma Eroica in tre atti — Poesia del ABBATE VARESCO

MUSICA DI

W. A. MOZART

The original version edited for performance by HANS GAL

Cast

Ilia, *a Trojan Princess, Daughter of Priam*	SENA JURINAC (*Jugo-Slav*)
Idamante, *Prince of Crete, Son of Idomeneo*	LÉOPOLD SIMONEAU (*Canadian*)
Arbace, *Counsellor to Idomeneo*	ALFRED POELL (*Austrian*)
Electra, *Daughter of Agamemnon*	BIRGIT NILSSON (*Swedish*)
Idomeneo, *King of Crete*	RICHARD LEWIS (*English*)
The High Priest of Neptune	ALEXANDER YOUNG (*English*)
The Voice of Neptune	BRUCE DARGAVEL (*Welsh*)

Conductor: FRITZ BUSCH

Producer: CARL EBERT

Designer: OLIVER MESSEL

Choreographer and Ballet Master: SIGURD LEEDER

Continuo by KAREL HORITZ, *Violoncello* and JOHN PRITCHARD, *Harpsichord*

THE GLYNDEBOURNE FESTIVAL CHORUS AND BALLET

Sopranos: MAUREEN ABBOTT, HELEN ANDERSON, KATHERINE BARBER, KATHLEEN BURROWS, SHEILA COWLAN, GIZELLA GONDOS-SMITH, STELLA HICHENS, ROXANE HOUSTON, RITA MCKERROW, SHIRLEY MANGER, INGRID MARSHALL, JOAN STUART, KATHLEEN WESTON.

Contraltos: HILDA ALEXANDER, THETIS BLACKER, PAMELA BOWDEN, PHYLLIS BRIDGWATER, MARY DAVENPORT, UNA FAIRFIELD, BARBARA GILL, JEAN GRAYSTON, NETTA GRIFFITHS, ENID HOLMES, EVE WARREN.

Tenors: JAMES ARMSTRONG, EMILE BELCOURT, JOHN CAROLAN, CHARLES DANSON, LEN JONES, CLIFFORD MILLAR, EDWARD MORGAN, BRYCHAN POWELL, CLEMENT ROSLING, CRAGG SINKINSON.

Basses: DESMOND CLAYTON, MERVYN DOBSON, GORDON FARRALL, JOHN HOBAN, TREVOR KENYON PHILIP LEWTAS, TERENCE MANT, STANLEY MASON, DAVID READ, JEFFREY SKITCH, DENNIS WICKS HOWARD WICKS, HAROLD WILLIAMS.

Dancers: SUSAN BARON, JOY BOLTON-CARTER, VALERIE LIDDELL, DALICE LLOYD, YOMA SASBURGH, NIGEL BURKE, HAMISH LIVINGSTON, COLIN PATERICK, JACK SKINNER, PETER WARWICK.

Glyndebourne has included "Idomeneo" in this year's Festival in memory of the late W. J. Turner (the distinguished critic of the *New Statesman*) who, before the war, continually besought us to perform this work.

apex of this arrangement, and when Richard made an expansive gesture I was a little too close and was almost wiped off the stage.

During the season most of us stayed around the area in the nearby village of Ringmer or in Lewes. I took a room in a pub called the Masons Arms and commuted by coach laid on from the station to the house.

Once again friendships were made with other singers and we enjoyed the use of the Green Room and gardens in our leisure time. We were relatively cut off from the rest of the world and became a very enclosed community as we concentrated on a life of rehearsals and eventually performances.

John Christie, the owner and founder, would wander into the theatre to watch, accompanied by his pug dogs. His wife, Audrey Mildmay, would also appear from time to time but I have only a vague recollection of seeing her.

I was invited to return the following year to take part in the first Verdi opera to be done at Glyndebourne, *Macbeth*, and also in Rossini's *La Cenerentola*, as well as the second season of *Idomeneo*. I decided to accept but that this would be for the last time, not wanting to become a regular chorister and needing to make progress with my career as a soloist.

It turned out to be an interesting season. As conductor we had the Italian Vittorio Gui, a very different personality from the German Busch, and a perfect choice for the Italian repertoire. The Rossini sparkled and shimmered under his baton, and every night I stood in the wings for the excitement of the overture, dancing with pleasure and anticipation. There is very little chorus in the opera – at least for the women – but it was thrilling to hear some fine coloratura singing from the cast: Marina de Gabarain from Spain in the title role – sadly to die young only a few years later; Juan Oncina, also Spanish, as an appealing Prince, and Sesto Bruscantini as a wonderfully comic valet. Ian Wallace was the father, and the ugly sisters were hilariously played by two emerging Italians, Alda Noni and Fernanda Cadoni, with finally Hervey Alan as the fairy godfather Alidoro. There was a scene where Cinderella is transformed into her costume to go to the ball and for this it was necessary to have a double to appear briefly on stage while she did a quick change. At one performance it fell to me to be the double, and as Marina was quite a lot taller, her cloak was much too long. I had to be led by Hervey upstage and had quite a job to prevent myself from tripping over the long cloak – all without prior rehearsal. Luckily the lights were dim so one hoped the audience was fooled.

The *Macbeth* preparations involved a great deal more with long, complicated chorus scenes, such as the witches in Act I and the great banquet scene. We also had to be a line of refugees – which led to something of a prank. We did a special performance of the opera for television and it so happened that in our dressing room I sat next to one of the dancers, Sylvia Ebert, Carl Ebert's daughter-in-law and wife of Peter Ebert, his assistant director. With them was their baby son – they went on to have a large family but this baby was the first and of course, spoiled rotten by all the cast. Sylvia and I decided it would add authenticity to our dispossessed status if one of us were to carry a baby. Without asking permission or warning our director, we duly bundled the baby in a shawl and during the shooting of the scene I carried him on. Bless him, he didn't murmur and we got away with it completely. Prof Ebert took it in good part and I believe it was the first time a baby had appeared in a live television performance.

An addition to the season in 1951 came with the company's first appearance at the Edinburgh Festival. We took up to Scotland Verdi's *La Forza del Destino*, playing at the King's Theatre. There was wide press coverage and we were photographed talking to visitors in Princes Street, playing a game of cricket against a city team (I was the scorer!) and playing croquet when I partnered Geraint Evans who was singing the role of Masetto in the other production, *Don Giovanni.* The orchestra during both seasons was the Royal Philharmonic and we got to know many of the players, some of whom were well-known soloists. Among the characters were Jimmy Verity, viola, Dennis Brain, horn, Jack Brymer, clarinet, Gwydion Brooke, bassoon, and many others.

Between and after these Glyndebourne seasons oratorio and concert work had been building up. I had also passed solo auditions for the BBC and given the first early-morning recitals – as one was expected to do by way of an apprenticeship. However, the very first recital was in the afternoon of 15 June 1951 and called 'May I introduce?', for which I received a fee of 7 guineas. Then followed the obligatory early morning recitals in January 1952 and August 1952 – the latter shared with the violinist Tessa Robbins. After that more sociable times were offered and gradually I became a frequent broadcaster.

Act II, Scene 3
Jamaica

IN 1952 MY FATHER HAD TO GO TO JAMAICA on business and offered to take me along for a holiday. I jumped at the chance and when it was known that I was to be there, the British Council offered me a recital in Kingston and some concerts in locations around the island. My parents and I travelled the slow route by Fyffes' banana boat from Liverpool to Kingston. The journey took about ten days and the boat was comfortably equipped for a dozen passengers. We sailed on 23rd December and spent Christmas Day being tossed about in the Bay of Biscay. I took to my bunk with fearful nausea after the first day and on Boxing Day my father sent the MO to my cabin with orders to get me up. The doctor gave me a monstrous pill that settled the sickness in no time and I was able to enjoy the rest of the voyage. The weather did not really clear up until we were in the Caribbean and about three days from our destination. We stayed for the first few days in Kingston where I gave my recital, heralded by the local paper the *Gleaner*, and with the co-operation of an excellent local accompanist.

The hall was set in the middle of the town, and although the concert took place late in the evening, traffic noise was something of a problem. One of the early items on the programme was a Handel aria, originally for soprano and violin obbligato, which I had transposed down to a comfortable tessitura and arranged the violin part into the piano accompaniment. It was entitled *Süsse Stille*, or *Sweetest Stillness* as I sang it in English translation. This turned out to be unfortunate on this occasion as the opening bars were accompanied by a fanfare of car horns from outside and there was considerable mirth at the opening phrase 'Sweetest stillness, kindest quiet, undisturbed serenity'!

It was all very well received and I enjoyed touring around the island seeing much of the countryside and places of interest – especially Montego Bay and Noel Coward's home. At a reception at the Governor's House, we heard the police band with their smart white uniforms and plumed helmets. Also present was the future Prime Minister, Norman Manley, to whom I was introduced – he shook my hand and said 'I can see you are a Conservative' – since

An evening with parents and friends: (left to right) Father, myself, Don Iddon (Daily Mail New York correspondent), Mother, Lord and Lady Graham

On the beach at Tower Isle Hotel, Jamaica

he was himself of the far left politically I was left wondering how he came to such an instantaneous decision – I hadn't yet said a word. He was then in opposition to Bustamante and was elected within a couple of years.

For the last part of our stay we moved to the north coast to the Tower Isle Hotel, set on the beach. My room's fourth wall was an open balcony on to the ocean, where a huge basket of fresh fruit was kept daily and breakfast served to the sound of breaking surf. There were sun loungers on the beach in the shade of coconut palms and we would watch boys shinning up the sloping trunks to collect the fruit. Staying at the hotel was a Hollywood film crew, on location to make a film starring Stewart Granger. He was unpopular among them for what they termed his arrogance and vanity, which was evident when he made a huge public row in the dining room one evening when asked to wear a tie. One charming actor in the cast was a character actor who appeared in countless films but whose name, Kurt Kaznar, was not well known. He was a friendly, cultured man who liked to talk about music. The chief cameraman took me to visit the set – a very interesting experience as in those days we knew so much less about the process of film-making than everybody knows today. Sadly I have forgotten the title of the film.

My career continued to expand with more important engagements coming along, including a BBC concert performance of Dvořák's *Rusalka* at the Royal Festival Hall under Rafael Kubelik in May 1954. The name part was sung by Gré Brouwenstein with whom I later sang several times. I sang the small role of Third Woodnymph.

Also in May I sang Bliss's *The Enchantress* in a BBC broadcast from Manchester, the first of many performances of that work. In June I first sang the role of Madame Larina in a TV production of Tchaikowsky's *Eugene Onegin* conducted by David Lloyd-Jones – more of this later.

This exciting year continued with another highlight – my first solo Prom appearance on 9 August singing the alto solos in Bach's *Magnificat*, conducted by Boris Ord. Bach with Boris was a great musical experience and the following year we worked together in a broadcast of the B Minor Mass (another first for me) followed by two further memorable performances at King's College Chapel, Cambridge. The BBC kept these recordings in their archives for many years but I gather they have now been scrapped.

Act II, Scene 4
Geneva

FOR SEVERAL YEARS Prof had been on the singers' jury of the Concours International d'Exécution Musicale in Geneva and indeed, in one year when he was not there, 1951, one of his students, Jennifer Vyvyan, a very talented soprano, had won joint first prize with Mattiwilda Dobbs (USA). It was early in 1954 when he suggested that I might be ready to try my luck and enter for the competition. We both felt that if nothing else it would be good experience for me and an opportunity to test myself in an international setting among singers from all over the world. We started to plan my programme according to the competition's requirements and would often try out this or that Lied or aria, decide it would not be ideal, and start again. We eventually selected from the best ones and then the careful preparation began.

First of all, everything must be memorised. Prof was insistent that no singer can communicate with an audience from behind a vocal score. In the case of the competition it was a requirement, but this was his dictum and became my own lifelong belief. The singer's facial expression and the eyes must be clearly seen by the audience if they are to transmit the emotion and the message of the song. The singer's imagination must be reflected not only in the voice but also in their body language and changes of expression, carrying the message of the poem and text if there is to be the closest rapport and communication with the listener. A singer needs to develop mobility of the facial muscles and to understand how changes in posture can affect the way the mood of a song is understood. After a time, these lessons are absorbed and the singer reacts instinctively to the feelings and emotions aroused in the song or aria – but this aspect of performance has to be studied as an actor studies a role.

We made quite sure that the tessitura (average level of the pitch range) of each item was comfortable for my voice and that each song struck a sympathetic chord in my own mind, imagination and musicality. For the opera aria, we selected *Kontchakovna's Cavatina* from Borodin's *Prince Igor*. For this it was necessary for me to sing in Russian so I went off to that formidable and incomparable lady, Oda Slobodskaya, who had been a great dramatic soprano. We worked together on the text, she beating on the piano and shouting in my ear with her great booming voice. I became very fond of her and she must have taught me well because, after hearing the aria, the Russian Nikita Magaloff, who happened to be in the audience, declared that I must have had a Russian grandmother.

Eventually the time drew near and I was lucky enough to be offered an evening with friends to sing through my programme, with Flora accompanying. It went well and they all sent me off with warm good wishes. On the day before departure was my last lesson with Prof, who invited one of his daughters to hear the programme. It was an unmitigated disaster. I was in dreadful voice, unable to find the mood of any of the items and feeling completely strung-up. Prof kindly said that of course a bad rehearsal makes a good performance but I was shattered and went home for a good cry.

Nonetheless, off I had to go the next day to Geneva where the organisers had booked me into a guest house a short tram ride from the centre. There several other aspiring competitors were staying, and we were generously and warmly looked after by our hostess, an excellent cook. The next three days were busy with rehearsals with my accompanist, Madeleine Depraz, who was a stalwart of the competition. I felt very comfortable with her and we saw eye to eye musically and artistically. The competition was in three sections: an elimination round where the jury were hidden behind screens and did not see the competitors at all; the semi-finals, where one had to perform a 20-minute recital; and the finals with orchestra. There were prizes for both male and female singers.

On the day of the eliminations we were gathered together in the hall of the Conservatoire from 2 pm, but since there were nearly 100 singers, some of us had a long wait. In fact, I did not get to sing until 10 pm. When at last my turn came I walked on to the platform and was told I could choose my own first item. Scarcely had we started the second one when a voice cried 'Merci, Mademoiselle', and that was it. Convinced that it was a total failure, I waited miserably for the results and was amazed to discover that my name was on the list to go forward to the semi-finals.

Gossip had it that a certain French soprano who had been sponsored by the French government had not survived the eliminations and that she, in fury, had been berating the administration and making a huge fuss. She had been confident of her chances and was mortified at the result. That particular singer went on to make a great career – a truly glorious voice which achieved a world-wide reputation. What went wrong on that day we'll never know and there is a lesson there for all ambitious singers.

Knowing quite positively that this would be my last appearance I booked my return flight for the day after the semi-final. The next day was free for rehearsals and I had my allotted time with Madeleine. The rest of the time was spent sight-seeing and sitting around in cafés with other singers. I had met a few others and become friendly, one being a Yugoslav baritone called Dusan Popovic. We had developed the habit of meeting at 11 am – not for ordinary coffee as usual, but for Turkish coffee and slivovitz, tutored in this by Dusan.

The semi-final recitals were held at the Victoria Hall and, as a contrast, my turn came early in the afternoon. I wore a beautiful black Spanish-style dress, three-quarter length with a tight lace-covered bodice fitting to the hips, then flaring out with layers of tulle. I walked on stage feeling, for once, very calm and absolutely prepared to sing my recital. The reception was enthusiastic and afterwards I was gratified by much praise and mobs of people wanting autographs. It was then that there appeared many new types, agents interested in signing me up, press wanting interviews, and just keen singing buffs.

Best of all, that day I met a couple who were to become lifelong friends, Frederick Fuller, the singer and language expert, and his wife Patricia. They were wildly enthusiastic about my performance and invited me next day to lunch at their apartment where they lived with their four daughters. I had heard of Frederick and admired his singing, so was enchanted to meet the family. We saw as much of each other as possible after that, wherever they lived in the world. At that time they were living in Geneva because Frederick was working as a translator at the United Nations.

Quite contrary to my predictions, I went through to the finals – and had to change the flight booking again.

There were three women and three men in the finals and we each had to sing one item with the orchestra, the Suisse Romande, in the Victoria Hall. My choice lay between the Bach aria *Erbarme Dich* from *St Matthew Passion* or *Kontchakovna's Cavatina*. I decided on the Bach but was unsure – was it sufficiently arresting for the occasion?

For the finals I wore a long white Greek-style draped dress with a halter neck. After the evening ended we all went to a nearby café to wait until the early hours for the results. I had been tipped as a possible winner but some felt that the serious Bach aria might have spoiled my chances, even though it suited me well. In the event, it hadn't, and I was declared winner of the Premier Prix Lauréat. I simply couldn't believe it – and events thereafter became a

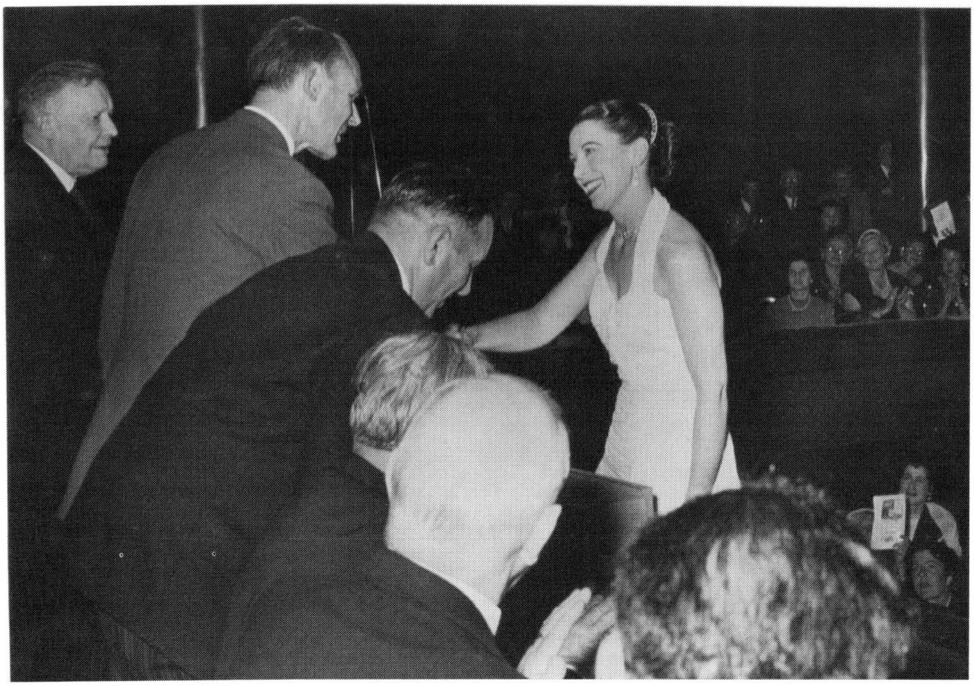

Receiving First Prize at Geneva, 1954

blur. There was a ceremony to award the prizes, and next evening a gala concert of prize winners, the orchestra conducted by the great Ernest Ansermet, long-time conductor of the Suisse Romande. I chose the Borodin aria this time. Our friend Dusan Popovic won the Premier Prix for men to our great delight. Second Prize for women went to Jeannette van Dyck, a charming Dutch soprano, and Third Prize to a bright little Italian soprano, Adriana Martino. Yet again my air ticket had to be changed as we were expected to give two concerts, one in Basel and one in Mulhouse, which were only memorable for the fact that all my money was stolen from the dressing-room while I was on stage at Mulhouse.

After the finals, all hell broke loose among the press – and even the English press, for the first time, heard about the success of an English artist; the *Daily Express* published a photo and article on the front page. Being unused to the ways of reporters, I had unwisely mentioned wishing that I had brought more evening dresses with me as we had to go on to give concerts. This was translated by them into a story of the poor girl who had only one dress. My mother rang in consternation asking if I wanted her to send some dresses out or

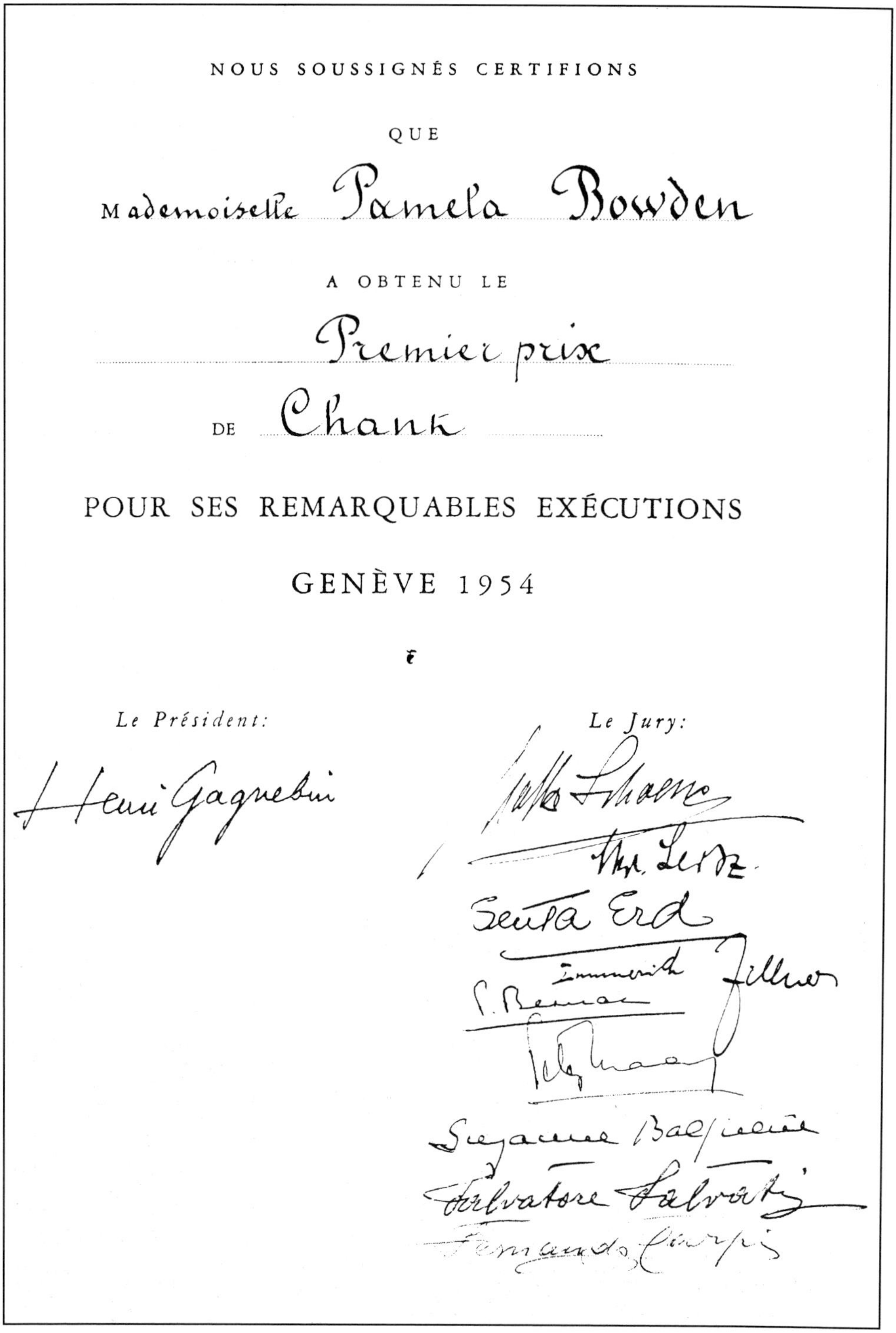

NOUS SOUSSIGNÉS CERTIFIONS

QUE

Mademoiselle Pamela Bowden

A OBTENU LE

Premier prix

DE Chant

POUR SES REMARQUABLES EXÉCUTIONS

GENÈVE 1954

Le Président:

Henri Gagnebin

Le Jury:

send some money to buy one. I reassured her that my dress would do very well for just three concerts and not to believe what she saw in the papers.

Among the bouquets of flowers was one, amazingly, from Gracie Fields. I was very touched that she had heard about her fellow Rochdalian and been kind enough to send congratulations. We later met in 1956 at the celebrations of the Centenary of the County Borough of Rochdale. A week of variety concerts was put on at the local theatre featuring 'Rochdale's own celebrities' – Gracie, comedian Norman Evans and myself each heading the cast for two evenings. My last meeting with 'The lassie from Lancashire' was when Derrick and I visited her and Boris at their home on Capri. Despite her reputation in the profession for being difficult, she always showed me the greatest kindness and we had a lot of fun and jokes.

Agents were ringing wanting me to sign contracts with them, but I decided to wait until the return home to take advice. In the end Ibbs and Tillett became my sole agents for many years to come. Decca offered me a recording contract which I was happy to accept.

After all the fuss and excitement in Switzerland, homecoming was a rapturous reception from family and a mob of press photographers at Heathrow. Arriving up in Rochdale for a rest, I came down with a horrendous cold and had to refuse an offer to appear on *In Town Tonight* because I couldn't croak a note.

With Gracie Fields at her home in Capri

EMILE LITTLER

GERrard 8202.

Palace Theatre,
Shaftesbury Ave.,
London, W.1.

Miss Pamela Bowden,
Quarry House,
Lower Healey,
ROCHDALE, Lancs.

16th October, 1954.

Dear Miss Bowden,

It is quite possible the substance of this letter will not appeal to you at all, in view of your happy prospects in the straight Musical world, but it is a suggestion from Mr. Emile Littler that I write to you.

Mr. Littler is presenting a Pantomime "THE BABES IN THE WOOD" at the Pavilion Theatre, Bournemouth for the Season of approx. eight weeks, as from December the 24th, and wonders if you might consider playing the part of 'ROBIN' HOOD' -- a dashing but very musically-vocal Principal Boy. We could not promise any Gold Medals at the end of the run, but you might care to consider a commercially attractive engagement.

Perhaps you will be kind enough to let me have your considered views.

Yours sincerely,

Fay Fisher (Sec.)

HASTINGS MANN.

After Geneva many doors opened!

Gradually things calmed down, the press and magazine interviews ended and we returned to something like normal – except that life was never to be quite the same again.

To receive suddenly so much publicity and attention, even at my advanced age of 29, was not easy to cope with. I had not expected to win any prize, certainly not First Prize, and I was foolishly unprepared for the consequences. Today there are many more international competitions and although winners do still receive a lot of attention, they are not subjected to quite the instant celebrity that came with the Geneva prize in those days.

I should of course be grateful for immediately being put on to a different standing from the growing national name that I had been making for myself – and indeed I shall never cease to marvel at the experience. In fact, though, I was put under immense pressure and from then on great things were expected – not easy to live up to, and one felt the relentlessness of the situation.

It was unusual for a singer winning an important prize not to be an opera singer. This had never been my ambition for two main reasons: firstly, there were few roles to which my type of voice was suited – I was not a dramatic mezzo to sing Delilah or Azucena or Eboli, nor had I the range for a coloratura mezzo role such as Cenerentola. Even the Mozart roles lay uncomfortably high in tessitura. Secondly, at that time I was not musically attracted to the grand opera repertoire of Verdi and Puccini. My tastes lay, and still lie, but now with much wider boundaries, with baroque and classical periods and with the song repertoire of all ages and nationalities. In other words I was a concert, oratorio and recital singer, with only occasional essays into certain

Prof's prize students – three first prizewinners of the Geneva Concours – Jennifer Vyvyan, James Milligan and myself

operas. I had no wish to join an opera company but was happy to sing the occasional concert version of Carmen or dip into arias for orchestral concerts.

Today it is infinitely more difficult to make a career as a recitalist and only a handful of specialist singers do so. Singers are obliged to be first and foremost opera singers and those who are able to sing recitals as well are perhaps in the minority. It has been said that the song recital is the apex of the singer's art and I agree that it requires the utmost skill and artistry to be able to create a different world for each song without the help of costume, make-up, scenery and other people on stage. The recitalist is alone, with only imagination, word-painting, variation of vocal colours and timbres, and the ability to transmit the composer's wishes to the audience, with the essential partnership of the accompanist as sole support.

Yet, what tremendous satisfaction when all this comes together and one is able to achieve those moments of true freedom and rapport with the poet, the composer and the listener. There is no greater joy – the more so because such moments are fleeting and unpredictable.

I have recently been shocked by the decline in standards of presentation among singers. It is no longer considered essential to memorise a recital programme and young singers do not bother to do so, having no compunction in having a music stand with scores in front of them for a whole programme. It is permissible to use the music, perhaps, for an ensemble piece with other singers or instrumentalists, or in the case of standing in at short notice, or performing a complicated new work. But in the case of a recital programme selected by the singers and booked well in advance, there is to me no excuse for not having adequately prepared the performance.

Apart from Mrs Langford and Prof, I sought some help from two others. One was Pierre Bernac, to whom I went briefly to work on French repertoire, visiting his home in Paris. He had heard me singing at Geneva and invited me to work with him. To this day I have his list of correct vowel formations and he was immensely helpful in attention to detail. The second teacher was Professor Frederick Husler whom I consulted, with Prof's agreement, as I was told he might be able to help me with the top of the voice. I went to his home near Hanover and stayed for several days on a couple of occasions, working on a new technique to free the upper voice using falsetto. His assistant, Yvonne Rodd Marling, became a friend and we later did a little work together in London. I did derive some benefit from it all and my voice became more flexible.

Act II, Scene 5
Travels Abroad

HAVING JUST DECLARED my lack of interest in singing opera, I must confess that the first thing my new French agent, Gabriel Dussurget, asked me to agree to was a series of performances as Orfeo in Gluck's opera *Orfeo ed Euridice*. This is one of the great alto roles and, with many reservations about my lack of stage experience, I decided to accept. The opera was to be given as part of the Festival de la Semaine de la Rose in Geneva in the summer of 1955. It was to be staged in the open air, but at exclamations of dismay, he assured me it would be 'sonorisé' and with a canopy over the stage in case of bad weather. No pity for the poor audiences, though.

He also invited me to sing the role of Cherubino at the next Festival of Aix en Provence in the south of France, of which he was Artistic Director. This I refused as neither Prof nor I felt it was the right moment for this role.

I set about learning the role of Orphée – it was to be sung in French, and up to that point I had only sung the famous aria *Che farò* in Italian. As it was sung in French originally in Gluck's time it felt comfortable and there were no problems committing the role to memory. To my relief the Act I aria which Gluck had added later as a show-piece was cut, since it bore little relevance to the plot or the dramatic flow of the work. My Euridice was the beautiful, tremendously experienced Janine Micheau, to whom I was everlastingly grateful for her support and help throughout what were sometimes fraught and difficult rehearsals. The main problem was that the German conductor, Günter Wand, and I did not get on – in fact we positively disliked each other, a situation I have never before nor since met and which I found profoundly disturbing as I sensed waves of antagonism wafting over the orchestral pit. The production suffered from acoustic problems with the open-air setting and I was surprised to discover the costumes were 17th century, mine being a long velvet cloak, tight-fitting tunic and tights, the former in heavy crimson velvet with gold frogging.

The costumiers clearly knew nothing about singers as they tried to pinch in my waist as if in corsets and I had to insist on it being let out further and further until it was possible to take a comfortable breath. A Greek robe would have been infinitely more comfortable.

The season was reasonably successful despite indifferent weather and we received good notices in the press. By the end of the run, the conductor and I had achieved an accord and when we met again, this time in Cologne for Mozart's *Requiem*, we managed to be, if not friendly, at least civil.

Among my friends in Geneva was Pierre Vidoudez, a maître-luthier, violin maker, with premises in the Old Town. He and his family invited me to their home and through them I met other Genevois music lovers. Pablo Casals was also a friend of theirs and spoke the most wonderfully Spanish-accented French that Pierre loved to imitate. I returned to Geneva on several occasions over the next few years, once to give a recital in a beautiful old church with Peter Gellhorn as accompanist, another time to give a concert of Bach cantatas with Gustav Leonhart at the harpsichord, again to record a concert for the radio, and again to give concerts with the Orchestre de la Suisse Romande conducted by Ernest Ansermet in Geneva and Montreux. He was by then a very old man and alas died soon afterwards. He was courteous and considerate, a great artist, and it was a privilege to work with him.

On one occasion I gave a recital in the Palais des Nations accompanied by my old friend Madeleine. We gave a programme of songs from many nations, and included Poulenc's *Le Bestiaire*, which the audience loved.

Together with Ron Golan the first viola of the Suisse Romande I gave my first performance of the Brahms songs for alto and viola which became a staple of the repertoire. The leader of the Vienna Philharmonic, Willy Boskowsky, came to one of our rehearsals and seeing him conduct the famous New Year's Day Strauss Concert in Vienna on television in later years took me back to that day.

I have always enjoyed travel and so it was exciting to be engaged to sing abroad. One early occasion was thanks to Nancy Evans. She had fallen ill and was unable to go to Cologne to the Nordwestdeutsche Rundfunk to record a contemporary programme of songs.

Ibbs & Tillett asked if I would be willing to take her place, the snag being that the concert would be in a week's time and the songs were not in my repertoire. However, not wanting to miss the chance, off I went. The radio station put a coach (pianist not transport) at my disposal and we got down to learning the songs, which were *Three Shakespeare Songs* by Stravinsky and *Chamber Music* by Luciano Berio, words by James Joyce. Both were accompanied by

Publicity photos from the 1950s and 1970s

instruments. It was challenging but certainly not impossible and we managed a successful and accurate performance. This was the start of other enjoyable visits to Cologne, where the coffee shops stocked the most fatteningly delicious pastries and the radio building had, in addition to the slipperiest floors I had ever experienced, one of those open, continuously moving lifts that were at first quite alarming to use. One wondered what would happen if one reached the top – did it turn upside-down to go down to the bottom again?

HOLLAND IS A COUNTRY that has always welcomed British singers and some of us were among the first to become regular visitors. The first trip to Amsterdam was to sing as soloist with the Concertgebouw Orchestra when one item was the staple *Kontchakovna's Cavatina*, with other arias. It was exciting to perform in that famous hall where, on another occasion, *Messiah* was the work – and what a strange mixture it was. There was a Dutch chorus and orchestra, a French conductor, Jean Fournet, who insisted the work be sung in German because he didn't like the sound of English!

The soloists were a Swiss soprano, Maria Stader, English tenor Alexander Young, Swedish baritone Kim Borg and myself singing alto.

Similarly another *Messiah* stays in the mind- this time totally fraught. It was to be in Zürich on Good Friday 1966. It was arranged that I should fly out on the previous Tuesday in time for piano rehearsal on the next day, full rehearsal on the Thursday in public, and performance on the Friday. My husband, daughter and au pair girl were to drive over on the Saturday and we were all to go down to Antibes in the south of France for a holiday. I, for some unfathomable reason, decided to take all my holiday clothes with me, and for once broke my rule of never packing jewellery. There was a muddle over flights at Heathrow, I had been given the wrong flight number and arrived too late although my luggage had been sent on a previous flight. I had to travel to Geneva, wait there for an onward flight to Zürich, so I took the opportunity to ring Pierre Vidoudez who drove out to the airport and kept me company while waiting for a couple of hours. On arrival at Zürich my suitcase was nowhere to be found. I had only my make-up case and clothes I was wearing. The next day, still no luck, nor on Thursday, so I had to make a rapid shopping expedition, being incredibly lucky to find, an hour before all the shops shut for Easter, the ideal black evening dress, shoes, jewellery and accessories.

My German score of *Messiah* had also vanished but that was easily replaced – I wasn't wholly confident of my memory of the German words, sorry to say.

To cut a very long story short, the suitcase never did turn up and I gave it up forever. Except: – ten years later, a letter came from a hotel in Verbier which had just changed hands saying that my suitcase had been found in their luggage room and what would I like them to do with it. When it arrived home, nothing much was any use except the music scores and a cherished address book given by Nancy Evans after the Cologne affair. The jewellery had long disappeared and the clothes were mouldy and well out of fashion.

GIVING CONCERTS AND RECITALS away from home can be a lonely business. One flies in to a city, locates the hotel, goes to rehearsal either with pianist or orchestra, back to the hotel, can't do too much sightseeing, if any, in order to reserve energy, meals often alone, then the performance, and off next day somewhere else.

Occasionally one has either more leisure time or happens to meet congenial people or old friends with whom to pass a few hours. A few such moments come to mind: there was a trip to Hanover to record a recital of Debussy,

Delius and Bliss songs. Staying in the same hotel were members of the Amadeus quartet and I always remember having dinner one evening with Martin Lovett, the cellist. Whenever we meet, as we did by chance recently, we remember that pleasant coincidence.

One curious event concerned a work that I performed on numerous occasions. The long scena for contralto and orchestra, *The Enchantress*, had been written by Sir Arthur Bliss for Kathleen Ferrier, who gave the first performance. After her death he asked if I would like to sing it in a series of concerts with him conducting the Bournemouth Symphony Orchestra. I enthusiastically agreed and revised the work, visiting his home in St John's Wood several times to go through it with him at the piano. He was a good pianist – but very loud, as he wanted to represent the full orchestration which was at times very heavy. Sir Arthur, Master of the Queen's Musick, was in appearance an upright, handsome man with white hair and moustache that made him look like a retired colonel. He was extremely kind to me, and over the years he and Lady Bliss would come to recitals at which I sang his *Seven American Poems*. He had worked on these songs with me and they became firm favourites, forming part of concert programmes as well as broadcasts.

A typically delightful letter from Sir Arthur Bliss

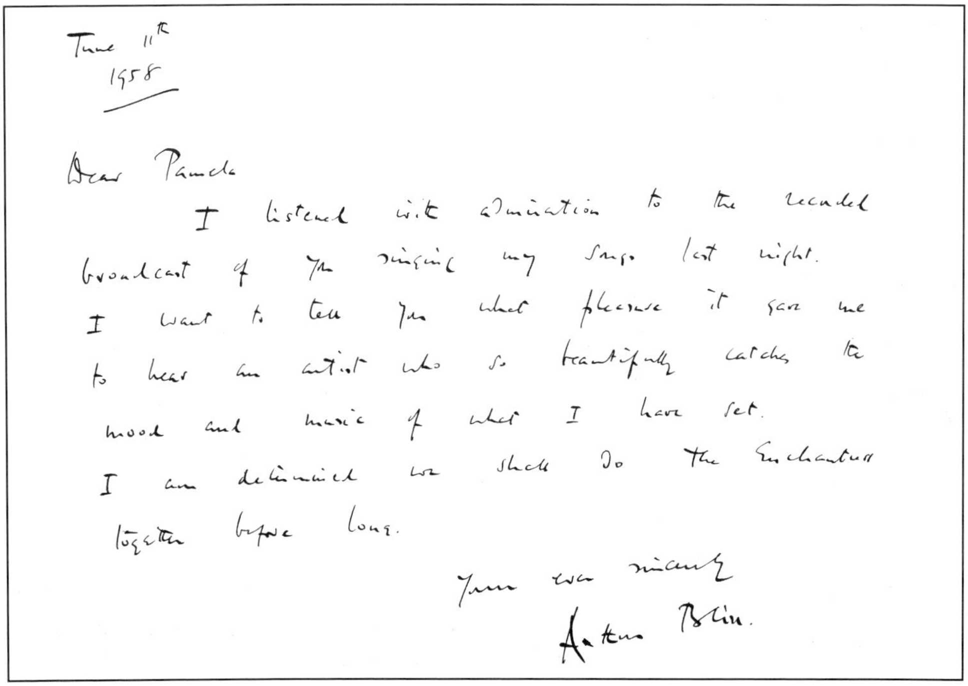
June 11th
1958

Dear Pamela

I listened with admiration to the recorded broadcast of you singing my songs last night. I want to tell you what pleasure it gave me to hear an artist who so beautifully catches the mood and music of what I have set. I am determined we shall do the Enchantress together before long.

Yours ever sincerely
Arthur Bliss.

On the strange occasion mentioned, I was booked to sing *The Enchantress* at two performances in Cannes during a summer festival of British music, with orchestra conducted by George Weldon, then conductor of the Hallé Orchestra. Also on the bill was the doyenne of English women pianists Moura Lympany playing the Rawsthorne piano concerto. We stayed at the same hotel and spent a lot of our free time together – I had admired her from afar and was thrilled to meet her. The weather was perfect, warm, cloudless blue skies, with the sea dark blue and sparking in the sun. A snag developed in the arrangements – the orchestral parts of *The Enchantress* had not arrived from London by the time of the first rehearsal and frantic phone calls revealed that they must be stuck in Customs. No amount of negotiating was able to get them to us by the time of the concerts and we were left with a dilemma. Bliss had specifically noted that the work must always be performed with orchestra – but a truly noble and generous offer from Moura to play the piano reduction for me was a lifeline. In the end we decided to take this course of action and Moura was an amazing strength and support in her inspired account of the score, sight-reading the complex music with ease and accuracy. Sir Arthur, when told of it later, did not blame us and agreed that to cancel the piece would have left an unacceptable hole in the programme.

THERE WAS A SHORT BROADCAST RECITAL TOUR in Germany in 1960 that stretched my stamina to the utmost. Being old enough and experienced enough by that time I should have known better than to accept my agent's outrageous schedule. It involved flying from city to city (Stuttgart, Frankfurt and Baden-Baden) to rehearse and record a thirty-minute recital programme on consecutive days, each with a different accompanist. By the end of five days I was voiceless and exhausted, and vowed never again to be so stupid. I was – but that's another story. A later visit to Baden-Baden allowed me to see a little more of the spa town as I was to sing a concert conducted by Paul Sacher. He gave me lifts in his Rolls-Royce, which had carpets of such depth that one's feet sank in it up to the ankles!

A less demanding trip involved visits to Norway and Sweden to record public concerts for the radio stations. The one in Oslo stands out for the fact that I briefly spoke to Louis Armstrong. He and his band were there for a concert the night I arrived, and he was standing beside me at the hotel reception desk as I checked in. Inadvertently – truly – I dropped my gloves and with a charming flourish he picked them up and handed them to me with a wide smile of gleaming teeth saying 'Here you are, ma'am'. What a pity I was too surprised to reply and get into conversation! That night my agent took me to the concert but I had to leave after half an hour as the level of noise was unbearable, not just of the music but the screaming fans. Luckily there was time on this trip to go to the top of the Olympic ski jump at Holmenkollen where there is a breathtaking view and heart-stopping idea of what faces the ski jumpers – terrifying.

On to Stockholm where another new experience awaited. The concert was before an invited audience and at the end the applause developed into a rhythmical slow handclap. I was horrified, thinking this conveyed disapproval but was hastily assured it was the opposite, and went on to sing a couple of encores.

It was flying back to London afterwards that, most exceptionally, I became totally deaf on landing. This might not have been too bad but for the fact that there was a concert that night at St Martin-in-the-Fields and I had to go straight to rehearsals. Instead of the ears popping as usual, they remained obstinately blocked and I had the very uncomfortable experience of singing unable to hear clearly – all was muffled and seemed miles away.

A singer needs the vibratory feedback into the ears and into the nervous system to be able to judge what he/she is doing. Quite apart from not hearing the accompanist, it is severely disconcerting to be receiving sound as though through cotton-wool.

ON THE SUBJECT OF DISASTERS and difficulties, there was one awful moment which I shudder to recall. Quite often I would be asked to sing in Copenhagen with the fine, established conductor Mogens Wöldike. One time we performed Handel's *Solomon*, myself in the title role, in an uncut version, restoring many of the arias and ensembles usually cut out of this long work. Mogens was a fine scholar and musician, and it was an especial pleasure to work with him.

However, on the occasion that I hate to remember the concert involved a performance of *Che farò* and the conductor was someone I had not met before – nor wished to ever again. We rehearsed the recitative before the aria and all went well. When it came to the performance, though, the first violinist forgot that the recitative was to be included before the beginning of the aria, and on the conductor's down-beat, started the introduction to the aria itself. The rest of the orchestra played the opening chord to the recit, but my ear was totally confused by the insistent violin melody. I sang something but it certainly wasn't Gluck. The conductor ploughed on instead of stopping and restarting as he should have, the violinist eventually realised his error – but the damage was done and what the audience, both present in the studio and on the radio, thought I can't imagine. What is galling is that on such an occasion, the singer would be blamed and I was later furious with myself that I hadn't just stopped singing and forced a re-start. A return to Copenhagen came later so they must have recovered from the shambles.

IN THOSE DECADES of the 1950s, 60s and 70s, as now, quartets of British singers would be booked together and one had the pleasure of the company of friends and colleagues for oratorios both in the UK and abroad. One of my most regular colleagues was the matchless and much-missed soprano Jennifer Vyvyan. We knew each other well; not only was she one of Prof's 'stable', but lived nearby, and after our marriages we both had our children at only a few months' interval. We became family friends and remained so until her untimely tragic death. We performed countless Messiahs together and her very fast tempo for *Rejoice greatly* was legendary. Sir Malcolm Sargent, with whom we both sang regularly, had a special marking in his score for her tempo: 'V fast for Vyvyan'.

In 1958, there was a special concert in Geneva to celebrate United Nations Day with a performance of Beethoven's *Choral Symphony*. Many, many other countries contributed to this worldwide event that was universally broadcast. A British contingent was booked, Jennifer and myself, plus tenor William Herbert and bass Owen Brannigan. We all travelled together and were photographed on the aircraft steps as we boarded the plane. This was an exciting event and marked I think, my own first performance of the piece.

Further Ninth Symphonies were also memorable. In December 1960 I was asked to go to Israel to take part in eight performances of the work with the Israel Philharmonic conducted by Josef Krips, in celebration of the 25th anniversary of the founding of the orchestra. At first I refused, as it would mean being away over Christmas and New Year, and I was newly-married and unwilling to be parted from my new husband. However, they extended the invitation to him to go with me, offering our own house, car and chauffeur. Naturally we said yes.

There were to be five performances in Tel Aviv, one in Haifa, one in Jerusalem and one in the kibbutz of Ein Gev on the Sea of Galilee. It turned out to be a great trip, my first visit to the Middle East, although my husband knew it well; he had served in the Royal Engineers throughout the North

African campaign in the war, and had visited most countries of the Mediterranean area.

Our colleagues were an American soprano, Theresa Greene-Coleman, Canadian bass Donald Bell and Australian tenor Ronald Dowd. Ron and Derrick hit it off at once and became firm friends which lasted until Ron and his wife went back to Australia in the 1970s. Ron had a wonderful heroic tenor voice and was a great Gerontius, which we sang together later.

Off to Geneva – to take part in the United Nations Day Concert and world-wide broadcast. On the aircraft steps at Heathrow: (back) Owen Brannigan, bass, and William Herbert, tenor; (front) Jennifer Vyvyan and myself.

EUROPEAN OFFICE OF THE UNITED NATIONS

OFFICE EUROPÉEN DES NATIONS UNIES

Télégrammes : UNATIONS, GENEVE
Téléphone : 33 10 00 33 20 00 33 40 00

REF. No. :
(à rappeler dans la réponse)

Palais des Nations
GENÈVE

4th August 1958

Dear Miss Bowden,

I have great pleasure in extending to you, on behalf of the Secretary-General, a cordial invitation to take part in the international concert to be given on October the 24th, United Nations Day.

As you know, this year's celebration promises to be an event of quite exceptional importance.

For the first time in history America and Europe can be linked by transatlantic music lines, so that the three parts of the concert, originating successively in New York, Paris and Geneva will be heard simultaneously throughout three continents.

Opening with the Boston Symphony Orchestra in New York, the international broadcast then turns to Paris where David Oistrakh and Yehudi Menuhin join in a performance of Bach's Double Violin Concerto. The Choral Movement of Beethoven's Ninth Symphony from Geneva will form the traditional climax of the celebration.

The participation of distinguished soloists from the United Kingdom in the performance of this great work is a source of particular pleasure both to Mr. Ansermet and ourselves, and will, I know, lend considerable lustre to the occasion.

The United Nations and the authorities of the City of Geneva look forward very much to welcoming you to Geneva,

Yours sincerely,

P. P. Spinelli,
Director of the European Office of the United Nations

representing the Secretary-General

The performances were remarkable for the fact that for the first time since the war the German language was used. At first we were threatened with learning the text in Hebrew, but later to our great relief German was allowed. A down-side of the trip was the number of incomprehensible, interminable speeches in Hebrew we had to endure at the many dinners and receptions in honour of the orchestra's birthday. We smiled bravely throughout.

Several incidents remain sharply etched in the memory. One was of our revered conductor leaning expressively towards the cello section at one point and falling off his rostrum, almost on to me! Another was when the soprano completely lost her voice in mid-flow and had to sit down for the rest of the evening. Afterwards Maestro Krips said to me 'My dear, well done! That is the first time I have ever really heard the alto part in this work'. Oh, the tribulations of the lower voices! The soprano had to withdraw from the rest of the tour and Elizabeth Simon flew out to join us from England. Jerusalem was divided at this time and we were unable to visit the important historical parts of the city, only to look out from the King David Hotel to see a panoramic view. We were fascinated by the barren scenery, punctuated by strips of irrigated and cultivated land which we travelled en route.

After a performance of Beethoven's Choral Symphony with the Israel Philharmonic Orchestra and Chorus, conducted by Josef Krips, with tenor Ronald Dowd, baritone Donald Bell and soprano Theresa Greene-Coleman

The kibbutz Ein Gev was full of interest and not a little danger. It was overlooked by the Golan Heights on top of which we could see Syrian troops and guns. Although it was nominally peace time, at any moment the inhabitants were prepared for shelling and attacks. There were shelters at the ready and we were instructed what to do if an alarm sounded. The concert hall was a huge metallic structure, packed to the roof for the concert, and the performance, as were all on the tour, was greeted with rapturous applause.

WE WERE ABLE TO SEE many biblical sites during our stay and visited Bethlehem and Nazareth. After the tour was over, Derrick and I stayed there for a short holiday, hiring a car to drive south to Beersheba and to explore a bit. We wandered around the ruins of Herod's Palace at Ashkelon and could pick up small pieces of ancient Roman tiles and of marble column. No attempt at preservation or archaeological research had yet been started. The souvenirs we kept were tiny and we liked to think that we didn't commit a serious violation of the site!

Driving past a Bedouin encampment, Derrick startled me by going right in – his experience of Arab hospitality told him we would be welcomed. And so we were, by a group of men in burnous and colourful head-dresses who offered us coffee – very strong and bitter – and a visit to the Sheikh's tent. This turned out to be a large area with faded patterned carpets and rugs, ancient settees and chairs around the walls, with photos of Victorian notables and the Sheikh himself with visitors. The effect was of a run-down Victorian reception

The kibbutz Ein Gev, on the Sea of Galilee

Michèle a few hours old – with Derrick on his way to race Aston Martins at Silverstone the same day

room. We were duly impressed and complimentary. Not a sign was there of a woman. The men asked us how many children we had and the answer none shocked them deeply. They couldn't understand how a couple of our age had only just married. We promised to get on with the creation of a family as soon as possible!

MY HUSBAND'S CAREER AND MINE made a most unlikely combination. Our marriage in 1960 had been heralded with headlines – 'Singer marries racing-driver' – and over the years people have been curious to know how we met. It was quite simple. After some fifteen years of Grand Prix driving all over the world, Derrick had realised it was time to think of the future and to start a business. He decided that as the Morris Minor was the most popular small car, he would open a garage specialising in them. This he did, in Belsize Park, and as I owned a nice little powder-blue Morris Minor, you can guess the rest.

He had not quite retired from racing so we used to try to meet whenever possible on our European trips. Once he was racing in Holland at Zandfoort while I was performing the Mahler cycle *Kindertotenlieder* with the Madrid National Orchestra conducted by Rafael Frühbeck de Burgos. After the two

Justin – a further fulfilment of our promise to the Arabs

concerts, I flew up to Paris in a small aircraft tossed negligently up into the sky and down again by a raffish Spanish pilot. Derrick met me at Orly and whisked me off to a favourite café where they made superlative rhum babas. We went on up to Zandfoort where I first met Roy Salvadori, the very good-looking and successful driver, and a number of other colleagues of Derrick's. It was a different world where the words 'music' and 'singing' caused people's eyes to glaze over. I learnt to separate myself from my own interests and to enjoy this largely masculine and macho world. Later I would become familiar with other race-tracks, driving around Nurburgring on a non-race day, Le Mans in France and of course, Silverstone and Brands Hatch in England.

Despite retiring from Grand Prix racing, my husband never stopping competing in vintage car races. He bought an Aston Martin of 1934 vintage which he lovingly restored and raced right up to his final illness in 1991. He became a leading light of the Aston Martin Owners' Club, having already been elected a member of British Racing Drivers' Club, an elite body of drivers and mechanics. We had many family weekends at race meetings and hill climbs. In return, he would come to my concerts as often as possible and was a lover of music and of opera. He couldn't bear contemporary music and I had to be careful not to subject him to anything too modern, for which he never hid his distaste.

His business changed its focus and developed into a specialist firm for restoring vintage Aston Martins. He met Nick Mason, the drummer of Pink Floyd, with whom he set up the garage in Kentish Town, and helped to build up a unique collection of beautiful cars. He was a workaholic and I remember arriving at the garage dressed in high style for a Royal Garden Party and having to drag him away to change out of greasy overalls into grey morning dress. We were unforgivably late in arriving at the palace on this occasion and Her Majesty was already in the garden – an awful breach of etiquette on our part.

Act II, Scene 6
Concerts at Home

IT IS TIME TO RETURN to the UK where the majority of my work took place in between the trips overseas. I have already mentioned singing often with Sir Malcolm Sargent. Indeed he was good to me and engaged me for countless Messiahs and other oratorio performances, including Proms. Much has been written about his personality, his unpopularity with orchestral musicians and god-like status with amateur choral societies, especially the ladies. He was a complex character with a brilliant mind, breadth of knowledge and a teflon-coated image. There was a radio programme entitled *The Brains Trust* on which Sargent used to appear as a member of an illustrious panel that also included the scientist Julian Huxley and philosopher Dr C E M Joad. Their weekly exchanges on topics that challenged their various expertises were brilliant, witty and informative, and Sargent could easily hold his own in such company. We got on well – he liked me because I was reliable, would know my work, and gave him no bad musical moments. I liked him because of his practical no-frills approach to rehearsing and his own reliability in always performing what we had rehearsed.

He was something of a control freak – everyone and everything on the platform under his baton had to be totally under his control. This extended, quite properly, to his insistence on us all knowing exactly how to behave on stage, exactly how the applause was to be acknowledged, in what order our bows were to be taken. For our oratorio performances there was a formal ritual to be observed, when he would bow, indicate the soloists, the orchestra and the choir. As a result his concerts always bore the stamp of professionalism and ran on oiled wheels.

This, however, led to an incident that caused me great amusement. It was on the occasion of a Royal Choral Society concert at the Royal Albert Hall, conducted by Sargent, at which I was engaged to sing the Brahms *Alto Rhapsody*. This is a work that I adored, a moving and deeply-felt piece, employing in the final section some glorious writing for male voice choir with superb vocal lines for the solo singer. I sang my heart out and gave everything

I had, excellently supported by the choir. At the end there was huge applause from a packed hall and for once I felt completely happy with a performance – not often did that happen. Sir Malcolm went through the usual formalities, shaking hands, all the usual bows, and then, as the applause was undiminished, I bowed yet again, only to hear a voice in my ear hissing 'Get off, get off'. I'm afraid I was enjoying myself far too much to obey, so I thought, 'Sorry, Sir Malcolm, not this time,' and took another bow. To his credit he never referred to the incident again and I cherish the memory.

Another happy memory concerns the time when Sargent was recording the Gilbert and Sullivan operas and he asked me to take the role of Mad Margaret in *Ruddigore*. I had not sung it previously, and was pleased when he suggested a run-through with piano early on the day of recording. We spent a half-hour going through the recit and aria and found that we agreed on the pacing and interpretation of the recit, with the aria being quite straightforward. I felt much more confident about the piece. As far as I can remember, the whole recording went through quickly and efficiently. We took the recit (*Cheerily carols the lark*), the aria (*To a garden full of posies*), the duet with Sir Despard, sung by Owen Brannigan, and the patter trio with Despard and Robin, sung by George Baker, in one take each with no necessity for a retake. The whole opera has transferred to CD very successfully.

The one area that to me was unutterably painful was to sing Bach with Sargent. He had a stylistic blind spot and, as in his Messiahs, would not acknowledge the growing trend for 'authentic' baroque performances with smaller forces, lighter and quicker tempi and clarity of texture. His Bach remained mired in 19th-century practice and he even insisted on piano continuo instead of harpsichord. He sometimes played this himself, which, though he was an accomplished pianist, was painful. His grand, grand Messiahs I could enjoy – somehow he brought great drama, dignity and breadth to them that held their own place against the interestingly different versions we used to experience with John Tobin and the London Choral Society.

John was the first to create and edit his own authentic version of *Messiah*, before Watkins Shaw published his, and his performances at the Festival Hall were the first uncut, four-hour long marathons. He used a counter-tenor soloist also for the first time and I remember sharing the platform with Alfred Deller who sang some of the alto solos and I others. I stood, all 5ft 4in, between Alfred and Hervey Alan, the bass, both well over 6ft, and felt very small indeed.

John Tobin was the first to embellish with ornamentation both the vocal lines and the orchestral parts, and he also wrote cadenzas for the soloists. Some of these lay well in the voice, others not so, but the time had not yet come – as it was later to do – when we had the confidence to create our own ornaments and cadenzas. He was an innovator and trail-blazer, and to my mind never received the credit due to him. He later gave his own editions of the Bach Passions – exciting, full of drama and eloquent.

Messiah was for me, as for most singers, our bread-and-butter work. Universally popular and guaranteed to attract full houses, choral societies all over the country, big and small, put on their annual performance. We sang in the same season with the Huddersfield Choral Society, with hundreds of voices; with little societies of less than fifty; with public schools and with grand London choirs such as the Royal Choral Society – and a huge variety in between. Every year the Belfast Philharmonic would put on a series of performances, sometimes three evenings running, and on one occasion even four. I used to go over for these when the troubles were at their height. Landing at the airport felt like arriving in a country at war. There was a palpable air of unease, of danger, as there used to be in war-time London. The soloists were all housed in separate hotels for security and we were not allowed on stage in the evening performances until after the National Anthem had been played in case of a bomb going off. The streets were patrolled by army jeeps manned by armed soldiers and all shops guarded at the entrance, handbags and shopping bags searched. One year, my dear friend, the soprano Ilse Wolf, was obliged every night to leave her bed and go to a shelter or stand outside in the street, because of a bomb alert at her hotel. I was luckier and enjoyed undisturbed rest. When I inquired the reason, I was told, 'Didn't you know? Your hotel is the IRA headquarters.' After that I looked with different eyes as I passed through the bar on the way to my room. The Belfast people we met were incredibly grateful to us for agreeing to go there to sing – but we felt we must do whatever we could to bring some comfort and relief into their lives.

At many performances the harpsichord continuo was played by a fine musician Philip Cranmer, whose father Arthur Cranmer had been a well-known singer, and whose family was descended from Archbishop Thomas Cranmer, the great reformer. Philip had a wonderful wit, and at one rehearsal, passed me a slip of paper on which he had written a limerick referring to the fact that we had just been rehearsing the middle section of 'He was despised', which spoke of 'shame and spitting'. It went thus:

A bright young contralto called Pam
Had not only a good voice but glam
She'd her solos by heart
Including the part
That talks about spitting and sham!

This was the first of others, and Philip and Ruth, his wife, became good friends. He was appointed Professor of Music at Belfast University and I stayed with them when invited over for concerts. Later on, when he was President of the ISM, he composed a very amusing collection of ensemble pieces entitled *Lloyd George knew my father*, which a group of us, including Peter Pears, recorded on LP and which was sold in aid of the ISM Benevolent Fund. It was very funny and extremely clever.

Another trouble spot we visited a few times was the city of Londonderry. Calm reigned during those days but stories abounded. The cathedral was the venue for our concerts and the nearby hotel famous for its charcoal grill open to the restaurant, where in full view they charred the most superb beef and ruined their lovely vegetables. I'm sure things have changed now!

SIR ADRIAN BOULT was another conductor for whom I sang many times during his reign as chief conductor of the BBC Symphony Orchestra. He was a man of contrasts with a charming, courteous manner, highly disciplined technique, and a reportedly volcanic temper that was most of the time kept strictly under control. He was a wonderful musician and a considerate colleague. Despite his celebrity he was incredibly modest and self-effacing. He travelled regularly by public transport (unlike Sargent who swept by in luxurious limousines) and on more than one occasion in my early days in the ad hoc chorus I would meet him and chat at a bus stop near Maida Vale studios on our way home after a rehearsal. Once, out shopping in the West End, I jumped on a bus and sat next to someone whom I soon recognised as Sir Adrian.

A fond memory arises from an evening in the sixties when we recorded a performance of *Messiah* in Studio 1 at Maida Vale in front of an invited audience. It all went smoothly, except that my first aria *O Thou that tellest good tidings to Zion* was rather slower than we had agreed at rehearsal. I liked a brisk tempo for this aria in order to convey the urgency and positive mood of the words. After the end of the recording, Sir Adrian came up and said, 'I'm so sorry, my dear, your tempi were a bit slow. These days I can't set a tempo after nine o'clock at night!' A lovely sense of humour!

Another regular *Messiah* performance took place in Glasgow on New Year's Day. This was hugely frustrating because, as the event started at 11 am, one naturally could not go out celebrating the evening before nor join the Scottish first-footers. The tenor on one Glasgow occasion was Peter Pears who was ever a kind, considerate and courteous colleague. I stayed with my dear friends Anne and Jim McTaggart in their large stone-built apartment near to the television studios where Jim worked. He was a great fan of the Modern Jazz Quartet and introduced me to their music. Years later I encountered the Quartet at an airport somewhere and memories flooded back.

James McTaggart was a remarkable man. He and Anne had met and married while they were both students at Glasgow University and while Anne (*neé* Donaldson, alias Maggie D – one of the six Wren friends) became a journalist, working for the *Glasgow Herald*, Jim joined the BBC, wrote and produced plays and made a fine reputation as an imaginative and innovative director. They moved to London where Anne became firstly editor of the Woman's Page, also theatre critic, and later Editor of the London edition of the Glasgow Herald. She was appointed OBE on her retirement.

Jim developed his career in television but was struck down by a heart attack and died tragically young. The BBC has honoured his memory with the McTaggart Lecture which is given annually at the Edinburgh Television Festival. Anne and Jim were my close friends and his death was a terrible blow. They had bought a charming old house at Kelmscott, quite close to the manor house which is now a William Morris museum, and we spent enjoyable weekends there. Anne kept the house on for the rest of her life and we had our Wrens 40th anniversary reunion there in 1984. We all managed a 50th anniversary reunion in 1994 at Pam C's home in Dulwich, but sadly Anne succumbed to Alzheimer's disease shortly afterwards and Maggie B died a few months later.

ONE OF THE MOST SPECTACULAR of all *Messiah* performances was given in 1970 under the baton of Yehudi Menuhin. The famous Willis organ at Alexandra Palace in North London, home of the first television transmissions back in the 1930s, had been saved by public protest from being sold off by the Greater London Council. To mark its reopening, the concert was planned by Haringey Arts Council using a choir of a thousand voices led by the London Philharmonic Choir, the Royal Philharmonic Orchestra, and soloists Jennifer Vyvyan, Ian Partridge, John Noble and myself. The hall was packed to the rafters and all would have been well save for the presence of a large pack of French paparazzi. Before and even during the performance, often at the most serious and profound moments, they would scuttle around in front of the platform, taking dozens of flash photos. It was incredibly distracting for those taking part and for the audience too, and it made one wonder how insensitive could these photographers be. In the light of their antics in later years, we have learned the answer to that.

Other concerts with Menuhin were much happier and enlightening experiences. It was a privilege to meet the great French musician and teacher Nadia Boulanger at Menuhin's home in Highgate, and to work with them both on a programme for the Bath Festival in 1967. Menuhin was then the Director of the Festival and the concert was given in the beautiful Assembly Rooms. It included Roxburgh's *Recitative after Blake* for voice and string quartet, a work that I had sung on many occasions. The concert was in honour of the 400th anniversary of the birth of Monteverdi and was directed by Nadia Boulanger.

A second visit to the Bath Festival came the following year when we gave a performance of *A Child of Our Time* in Wells Cathedral, with Tippett himself conducting and Menuhin playing the Brahms Violin Concerto conducted by Nicholas Braithwaite.

THERE WERE, OF COURSE, many other oratorios in the repertoire such as Mendelssohn's *Elijah*, the Mozart Masses in C minor and C major and the numerous Haydn Masses, such as the *Nelson* and the *Missa in Tempore Belli*, in which I was one of the soloists in a recording made in King's College Chapel, Cambridge, conducted by David Willcocks. There were also Handel oratorios such as *Jephtha*, *Samson*, *Solomon* and others that today are sometimes staged and treated as operas. Then there were modern oratorios of the 20th century such as *A Child of Our Time* and Honegger's *King David* – of which I have some great memories of singing on some performances conducted by Sargent in Leeds and London, when the Narrator was Richard Attenborough, who entered into his role as the Witch of Endor with such verve that he very nearly rendered himself speechless. Joan Sutherland was the soprano, at that time still singing the weightier soprano roles and not yet discovering her fabulous *bel canto* style.

There were two works that I came to after some time. The Verdi *Requiem*, if performed as it should be with large forces, required sizeable voices and it was not until I was in the mid-thirties to forties that I felt able to tackle it. It was worth the wait and I came to look forward eagerly to each performance.

So gratefully
Nadia Boulanger
June 13th 1967

Thank you
Yehudi Menuhin

1967 Bath Festival
Artistic Director: YEHUDI MENUHIN

Tuesday 13 June at 8 pm
Assembly Rooms

A concert in honour of the 400th anniversary of the birth of Claudio Monteverdi

Janet Price, Maureen Keetch, sopranos
Pamela Bowden, Elisabeth Holden, contraltos
Roger Norrington, Duncan Robertson, tenors
James Atkins, bass

with

Yehudi Menuhin, Joseph Fuchs, Eli Goren, Peter Thomas, violins
Patrick Ireland, John Davis, violas
Bruno Schrecker, Ross Pople, 'celli
Michael Brittain, bass
Michael Dobson, oboe

Directed by Nadia Boulanger

DOWLAND	Lachrymae Antiquae: The King of Denmark's Galliard
TALLIS	O Nata Lux
BYRD	Ave Verum Corpus
GILLETT	Rhapsody for Oboe with viola and soprano voice obligato Michael Dobson, oboe with Janet Price, soprano Patrick Ireland, viola
ROXBURGH	A Recitativo (after William Blake) for voice and string quintet Pamela Bowden, contralto
	Interval
BACH	First Sonata for Violin Solo Yehudi Menuhin
MONTEVERDI	Hor Ch'el Ciel Quel Sguardo Ecco Mormorar L'Onde Damigella Tutta Bella T'Amo Mia Vita Chiome D'Oro.

LANSDOWN GROVE HOTEL,
BATH.
TELEPHONE: BATH 5891/2.

All the best
for this
evening
devotedly
Yehudi
Menuhin

The Bath Festival programme for 13 June 1967 – and Yehudi Menuhin's note to me before the performance

Elgar's oratorio *The Dream of Gerontius* was another work I started performing later in my career as its vocal and emotional demands needed experience and maturity. There are great memories of outstanding interpreters of the title role, including Richard Lewis and Ronald Dowd. One particular day is memorable for amusement given to the choir. The journey to Harlow, in Essex, for the rehearsal had been fraught with delays, and I arrived a little late. As I entered the hall I heard the music leading up to my first entry as the Angel, so walking in and peeling off my coat, I sang the opening words, 'My work is done, my task is o'er; and so I come, taking it home, for the crown is won. Allelujah!' At which point, the rehearsal collapsed.

WHEN IT CAME TO LAUGHTER, nothing could compete with the famous Hoffnung concerts at the Royal Festival Hall. The Hoffnung Astronautical Music Festival took place in 1961, and included the world première of *Horrortorio*, a work specially written for the occasion by Joseph Horovitz. I created the grand role of the Dowager Baroness Frankenstein. Recordings of this went on to the market soon afterwards and the fun we all had lives on. Each item in the concert was a masterpiece of wit and satire, with no small ingredient of erudition – all following the tradition established in the former Hoffnung Festivals in 1956 and 1958.

I FIRST MET BENJAMIN BRITTEN in 1955 when I was to record his songs *A Charm of Lullabies* for Decca, with Peter Gellhorn accompanying. I asked Ben Britten if he would kindly hear me sing them and he invited me to his apartment where he accompanied me and coached me in his exact preferences for their interpretation. It was a great thrill to learn from him and to have the experience of his matchless accompanying.

A few months later I received a charming letter from Ben asking if I would be willing to sing the solo part in the first performance of a new work by Hans Werner Henze entitled *Apollo und Hyazinthus* at the next Aldeburgh Festival. It was a largely orchestral piece with a short but important solo. I was thrilled to accept and the performances took place in the old Jubilee Hall – the Maltings had not yet been built. The BBC broadcast one performance and the composer was present. The Duke of Edinburgh paid a flying visit too.

In 1958 an invitation came to take part in the Aldeburgh Festival in a Bach Cantata, a broadcast concert, and to sing the role of Venus in Monteverdi's *Il Ballo delle Ingrate*. This was a role I had already performed at the Hovingham Festival so I was quite comfortable with it. What made it particularly

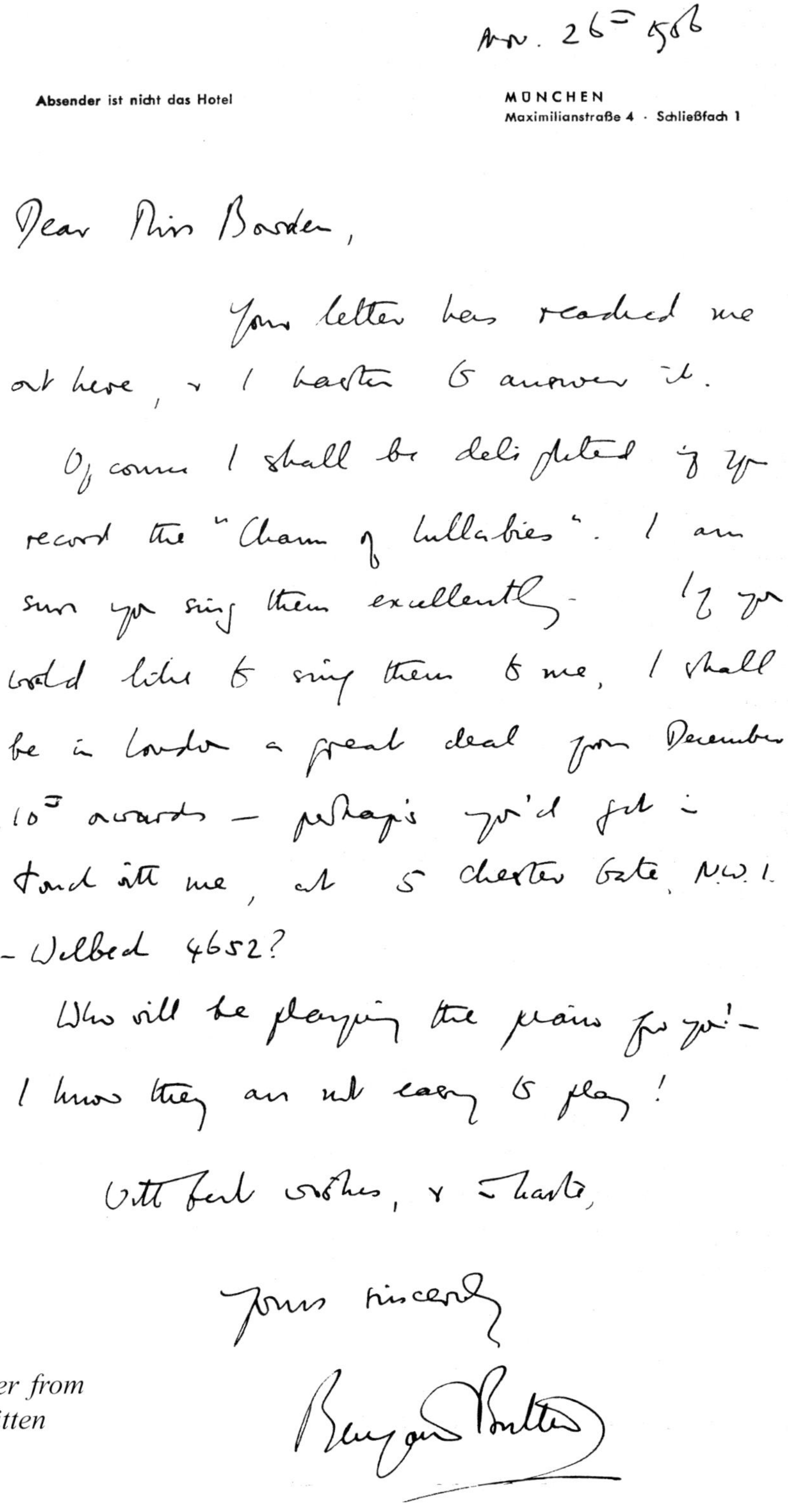

Nov. 26th 56

Absender ist nicht das Hotel

MÜNCHEN
Maximilianstraße 4 · Schließfach 1

Dear Miss Bowden,

Your letter has reached me out here, & I hasten to answer it.

Of course I shall be delighted if you record the "Charm of Lullabies". I am sure you sing them excellently. If you would like to sing them to me, I shall be in London a great deal from December 10th onwards — perhaps you'd get in touch with me, at 5 Chester Gate, N.W.1. – Welbeck 4652?

Who will be playing the piano for you? — I know they are not easy to play!

With best wishes, & thanks,

Yours sincerely

Benjamin Britten

The first letter from Benjamin Britten

interesting on this occasion was that the designer was the painter John Piper. He gave me a luscious blonde wig, insisting that Venus must be a blonde, and a flowing, gauzy dress. A new skill too had to be mastered – how to walk down a flight of black steps with a spotlight on my face, unable to look down and see where to put my feet, singing the while. At the first dress rehearsal John Piper leapt up on to the stage from the stalls, brandishing a large pair of shears, and proceeded to cut my skirt into ribbons. At my alarmed reaction he said 'Don't worry, we'll give you flesh-coloured tights and you'll be perfectly decent.'

Sadly this marked the end of my engagements at Aldeburgh, suddenly and for no apparent reason. This was not unusual in the annals of many singers' experience with Britten – he would frequently drop artists from his favour and there are many who couldn't understand the reason for their rise and fall in the Britten orbit. There were of course a special few who survived much longer and became regular Festival artists, but they were very much the favoured few. I was not too upset at being dropped because, first of all, I knew about this tendency, but also because I found the whole atmosphere at Aldeburgh claustrophobic and neurotic; I did not feel comfortable while working there and couldn't wait to get the job done and get away again.

There were moments to look back on with pleasure, such as attending the first performance of *Noye's Fludde* in Blythborough Church – a magical and inspiring occasion – and a garden party at The Red House, Ben and Peter's home.

Contacts with royalty were not particularly frequent but there were times when, like many singers and other musicians, our concerts were attended by, or patronised by, members of the royal family.

One occasion was in 1959 when I sang at a Royal Concert, part of the St Cecilia's Day celebrations, at the Festival Hall, singing the Pigeon's Song in Bliss's *Pastorale* with the Bournemouth Symphony Orchestra and choir conducted by Charles Groves. The concert was attended by the Queen Mother and we were presented in the interval. Dame Myra Hess was the soloist in Beethoven's Fourth Piano Concerto. I remember wearing a gorgeous red satin dress designed for me by an artist called Clarence Wilson whom I had met among a group of young painters. He designed a number of evening dresses for me before emigrating to South Africa, leaving in my care a large painting which he would reclaim on his return. As far as I know he never did come back and the painting still hangs in my hall to this day.

Charles Groves, later Sir Charles, was one of the finest 'singers' conductors'. His early training and experience as a chorister had given him understanding of the voice and great sensitivity in using the orchestra as accompaniment. He would instinctively breathe and phrase with the singer, always creating the mood and colour of the text. I was one of the soloists in a performance of Bach's *St Matthew Passion*, which was his own first time of conducting the work. It was an intensely moving performance, heartfelt, dramatic, expressive and unforgettable for those who took part. A great experience and a cherished memory.

I HAVE ALREADY MENTIONED singing the role of Venus in *Il Ballo delle Ingrate* at Hovingham Festival. This took place in 1955. The Festival was a week of concerts and opera based at Hovingham Hall in Yorkshire, the home of Sir William and Lady Worsley, parents of Katherine, the future Duchess of Kent. I was invited to stay with them and enjoyed a delightful week of rehearsals and performances. The conductor of the opera and musical director of the festival was Professor Stuart Deas of Sheffield University, with whom I was to sing many times over the years.

The Worsleys were charming hosts, with wide cultural interests and owning some great paintings. Their two sons, Marcus and Oliver, also entered into the festival with enthusiasm and I kept in touch with Oliver for some years afterwards. The countryside was beautiful with soft hills and dales and the prettiest villages. Often after rehearsal I would don a pair of wellies and be shown around the estate, see the prize bull and the pigs, or go for walks around the lanes. Sir William was a keen cricketer and President of the Yorkshire Cricket Club, which he took very seriously. Lady Worsley was a rather shy but charming person.

The late Princess Royal attended some of our performances. Her eldest son, Lord Harewood, was of course involved in music all his life and I came across him several times. One interesting occasion was to be invited to sing the mezzo part in Janáček's *Diary of One who Disappeared*, to be performed at Harewood House. Also in the programme were the wonderful Schumann songs Poems of Mary Queen of Scots, which I sang accompanied by Roderick Brydon. We were invited to stay at Harewood House, near Leeds, where we prepared for the concert. The tenor, who has the major role in the work, was Vilem Přibyl, a fine heroic tenor who sang at Covent Garden. We were to sing the work in Czech, which was of course Přibyl's native tongue. I had to learn my part phonetically – not ideal, but there was hardly time to learn the language as well. Vilem coached me in the pronunciation,

Beethoven's Missa Solemnis in York Minster, with conductor Hans Schmidt-Isserstedt, William Blankenship, tenor, Elizabeth Söderström, soprano, and Kim Borg, bass

which wasn't so much difficult as almost impossible to sing, consisting of strings of consonants and few vowels. As one always remembers unimportant details, I remember the first lunch at Harewood, when we were given shepherds pie, allegedly George Harewood's favourite, and Hungarian wine Bulls Blood!

A second Hovingham Festival was held the following year and we all hoped that it might become a regular annual event, but alas it was not to be – possibly it entailed too much work to be sustained on the largely amateur basis – but it was a lovely example of what can be achieved in a very English setting. I met them all again the same year while taking part in a performance of the Monteverdi Vespers at York Minster, conducted by Norman Del Mar – an inspiring performance in that wonderful setting.

York Minster was a favourite concert venue. Another occasion there involved the celebrated conductor Hans Schmidt-Isserstedt in a performance of Beethoven's *Missa Solemnis*.

Festivals of one sort or another played quite a large part in British musical life, and in my life. One of the most important – and least well-publicised –

was the Three Choirs Festival. It is still flourishing, circulating annually between the three cathedral cities of Worcester, Hereford and Gloucester. I sang at all three on numerous occasions and always enjoyed the atmosphere, the hospitality, the choral concerts and also the opportunity to meet other singers whom I did not normally encounter.

One example of this was meeting other contraltos, and there was an occasion when Norma Procter and I were walking down the street together, to be accosted by a lady who said something to the effect that how amazing it was to see two 'rival' contraltos together! Norma and I thought this very funny as we were good friends, both Roy Henderson's students, and on excellent terms. I never felt great rivalry with other singers – perhaps envy of those who got concerts I would have liked to do – but no real bitterness. We were all so different from one another and had totally different voices and musical and artistic assets to offer. Rivalries exist very strongly in opera companies and throughout the operatic world – which is one reason why I never wanted to join an opera company, other than for short, guest appearances, much preferring to keep myself free, able to come and go as I wished, and have a life unencumbered by such pressures.

Act II, Scene 7
Ballet

THE OPERA FESTIVAL AT WEXFORD has existed for many years, largely famous for its presentation of unknown or rarely performed operas and often engaging little-known foreign singers. It takes place in the small town of Wexford in the Irish Republic in a tiny theatre which, in the 1960s, was not particularly comfortable for the audience and incredibly cramped for the performers. In 1967 I was invited to sing the small role of the Nurse in Gounod's *Roméo et Juliette*, conducted by David Lloyd-Jones. Among the company were Michèle Raynaud as Juliette and Jean Brazzi as Romeo, with Richard van Allen as the Duke of Verona and Anne Pashley as Stephano. After accepting the role, however, an invitation came from Covent Garden to sing several performances of *Das Lied von der Erde* – Mahler's great work for mezzo and tenor soloists and orchestra. This was to be performed as a newly choreographed ballet by the Royal Ballet in a double bill with *Marguerite et Armand*, the star vehicle for Fonteyn and Nureyev. The huge snag was that the dates were in precisely the same period as the Wexford opera performances. I was frantic! Not only did I want to have an opportunity to sing the Mahler again – there had been my first performance of it at the Festival Hall in 1957 with tenor William Herbert, conducted by Hans Swarowsky – but I was also enchanted by the thought of appearing at Covent Garden, even if it was not with the Royal Opera, and at the prospect of seeing those fabulous dancers at close quarters. After looking closely at the opera and ballet dates, I realised that there was a way to do both – but only if I were completely mad and only with the most incredible luck. Well, in fact both of these conditions came true in the end.

The engagements fell on alternate days, so I would for example, do the Gounod one evening, drive a hired car to Dublin airport the next morning, fly to Heathrow where my husband would meet me and take me home. That evening I'd sing the Mahler at Covent Garden and the following morning, Derrick would drive me to Heathrow to catch the plane to Dublin, pick up the car, drive back to Wexford, sing that night in the opera – and so on, and so on. Where luck held was in the reliability of the flights and the good weather.

Nothing went wrong and the week passed like a dream. But it could have been disastrous and nobody should really take such risks.

The Mahler was very exciting to do in combination with the ballet. The conductor was John Lanchbery. The tenor (Kenneth Macdonald) and I stood on either side of the stage to sing our movements, three each, while the ballet was danced behind us. Among the cast were Anthony Dowell and Monica Mason. Alas, we never saw it properly and have no idea what was going on on the stage. From our point of view it was not the most satisfying musical experience. The balletomane public is on the whole very single-minded, even blinkered, and did not appear to be at all interested in the musical quality and artistry lying behind the music to the dance. Our audiences, and even the critics, could not have been less involved in the settings of the poems, translated from the Chinese, that Mahler had chosen to use as the vehicle for his symphonic work. I did not see one notice in the papers that mentioned either the tenor or myself, or that any singing had been part of the performance. Ah well – that's life. I did, however, get to meet Margot Fonteyn whom I idolised, and was even more thrilled with her in person.

This close-up of the ballet dancers at work made one realise how extraordinarily tough is their life. Standing in the wings, seeing their thistledown leaps and arabesques, seeming so effortless and graceful, then finding sweaty, panting bodies rushing past one to bend over gasping, only to recover seconds later to return as poised, collected dancers on stage. Later that year we repeated *Das Lied von der Erde* in double bill with *Shadowplay*, a ballet by Anthony Tudor to music by Koechlin.

THIS IMPRESSION WAS REINFORCED by the next contact with the ballet in 1969 when once again I was asked to sing with a group of dancers, this time the London Festival Ballet, at that time administered by the redoubtable Beryl Gray. This time it was to be in Paris during the summer at the Festival du Marais. It was held in the old district of Les Halles, recently vacated by the market, and the Festival's objective was to raise money to refurbish and save the old buildings of the neighbourhood. My role in this was to sing in performances of Berlioz's *Les Nuits d'Eté*, a cycle of six songs with orchestra, to which a ballet had been created. I was asked to do it at quite short notice and, not having sung all the songs before, had to do a quick-learning exercise, shut away in a small bedroom in a little hotel in the Palais Royal with score and cassette recorder. The performances were something of a trial. Although supposedly summer, the weather was poor, chilly and wet, and the huge old ex-market building in which a temporary theatre had been created was unheated and incredibly draughty, with panes of glass missing from the vast expanse of glass roof. Once again I stood at the side front of stage to sing while the ballet was performed behind me, and once again I saw nothing of the action! As usual, the music and musicians took second place and, astonishingly, in the programme the music was attributed to Verdi. The stars of the ballet were Galina Samsova and André Prokovsky and the conductor Terence Kern.

The dancers were delightful, very friendly, and each night after the performances we would all go to the nearest restaurant for a meal, starting of course with the local speciality onion soup, which used to be the staple of the market traders. It was wonderful, dark brown and thick with onions and a crust of cheese. The dancers would stay late, talking and drinking, knowing that they would have to be up early next morning for class, followed by rehearsals and work most of the day, whereas I could rise late, take my leisure and only think about preparing for the next night later in the day.

Just to finish the ballet connection, my very first contact came in 1955. Berlioz's *Roméo et Juliette* is an extended orchestral work with solos for mezzo, tenor and baritone. It is a concert work but provides a fertile field for translation into a ballet, which is just what George Skibine, John Taras and W Skouratoff created for the Grand Ballet du Marquis de Cuevas.

They called it an opera-ballet, and put on five performances in the courtyard of the Louvre in Paris during June and July. This was of course before the pyramid was built there to ruin, in my opinion, the wonderful classic proportions of the buildings and their central space. Staging was built against one side of the courtyard, rising in three levels to the topmost windows. On the ground was the orchestra, at first level Friar Lawrence's cell, on the second, the town, and third top level was Juliet's balcony.

My colleagues in this were the baritone Michel Roux, tenor Michel Sénéchal, and conductor Jean Martinon. As I was once again the Nurse, I had to sing from the topmost level, a very long way up indeed. Getting there was no problem as French windows opened from a salon on to the stage, but seeing the conductor was! When I looked over the edge of the rather flimsy staging, I could see the tiny figure of the conductor way below. But there was a considerable aural delay. Jean Martinon obligingly wore wide white cuffs and gestured high into the air for my benefit when I sang. It was a memorable affair – the opening night saw huge pomp and ceremony in traditional French fashion with an audience of high officials and guests, government ministers and VIPs of all kinds. There were fireworks, fanfares, the National Guard out in force in dress uniforms, the lot.

The best thing for me, though, was the costume. Apparently the costumes were hired from film costumiers and my own dress at the first fitting turned out to be huge, obviously made for someone much taller and broader. It completely swamped me and had to be considerably altered to fit. It was with delight that I discovered sewn into it a label with the name 'Nurse – Flora Robson'. She must have worn it in the old film of Romeo and Juliet which I remember seeing many years earlier. I felt hugely gratified to wear the same dress as that great actress and she must have helped me to get into the part – or so I liked to think.

ALTHOUGH I NEVER TOOK PART in Stravinsky's *Les Noces* with a ballet company, the music was written for a ballet and therefore a reminiscence of it fits in here. The work is scored for four pianos, percussion, four solo voices and chorus, and I was asked to sing the solo alto part in concert performances at the Royal Festival Hall conducted by Pierre Boulez. It is fiendishly difficult with its insistent stabbing, constantly changing rhythms and plethora of Russian words. It was hard work to get the piece into one's system, knowing Boulez's reputation for inflexible, metronomic beat. When we met for rehearsal it was a little disappointing that he had very little to say to the singers, seemingly concentrating on keeping the pianists and company together – a none-too-easy feat. It was encouraging at the performances to discover that he, too, is human and became excited enough by the music to allow the tempo to run away with him at times!

We subsequently did another performance of the work at the Royal Albert Hall which I vividly remember for a family reason. My little daughter and her au pair (an ardent music lover) were in the stalls during rehearsal and they listened to the whole thing. Some weeks later I was in the car with Michèle on the back seat, happily humming to herself. I was staggered to recognise themes from *Les Noces* and began to believe my daughter to be a musical genius in the making. In fact, it just helps to prove that little children are musical sponges and there should be far more attention paid to developing and encouraging them while still very young. As a tail-piece to this anecdote, I recently watched with great interest a TV transmission of *Les Noces* from the Royal Ballet. At the end the credits rolled and were also spoken by the presenter. All the dancers' names were given, the conductor and all the pianists were named – not a word was said about the solo singers. Don't tell me they ran out of time.

Act II, Scene 8

Pianists and Composers

SO FAR I have not made mention of pianists, except in passing. Perhaps it was due to early upbringing that I have always had a fondness for the piano and rapport with pianists – not only because for a singer, the accompanist or coach is such an important and essential colleague, but also because piano music is such a vast and rich source of musical delight. One has to admire and respect the dedication and sheer slog that is part of the life

Programme

Altisidora's Song (Don Quixote)	PURCELL
Lied der Mignon Suleika Der Tod und das Mädchen Der Musensohn	SCHUBERT
Le Jet d'Eau Le Temps a laissié son Manteau	DEBUSSY
Phidylé La Vague et la Cloche	DUPARC
Prison	**FAURE**
INTERVAL	
Le Bestiare Le Dromadaire La Chèvre du Thibet La Sauterelle Le Dauphin L'Ecrevisse La Carpe	POULENC
Seven American Poems Gone, gone again is Summer Siege Feast Little Elegy Rain comes down Fair Annet's Song Being young and green	BLISS

The programme of my first Wigmore Hall concert, in 1955 (see opposite)

of a concert pianist in whom a virtuoso technique is today taken for granted. Of accompanists scarcely less is required.

The longest and closest collaboration was with my friend and colleague of long standing, Flora Kent, who was like, if not a mother to me, certainly an elder sister. Always ready with support and encouragement, Flora was a sympathetic and knowledgeable accompanist who was universally popular with singers and instrumentalists alike.

Besides playing for Prof on a daily basis, she also accompanied at music festivals and at concerts. She played occasionally with the violinist Alfredo Campoli – these concerts cost her sleepless nights and many hours of practice to achieve the high standard he demanded. Flora accompanied me for many of my early concerts and even for my first Wigmore Hall recital in 1955.

Unfortunately she was unable to give of her best as she was suffering from a severe attack of nervous exhaustion that lasted for months. She battled bravely on and still managed to hide until much later how ill she had felt.

The second Wigmore Hall recital (1958) was accompanied by Gerald Moore in a programme which included a group of early Italian songs, four Mahler songs, a group of Spanish songs by Turina, de Falla and Nin, then *A Charm of Lullabies* and ending with some French folk songs arranged by Antony Hopkins. Gerald was as ever a brilliant and supportive duo partner.

My third Wigmore Hall recital in 1960 was accompanied by Peter Gellhorn with whom I worked over many years. This programme was given in aid of World Refugee Year and included an early group of Mercadante, Handel and Purcell, the *Three Greek Songs* by Lennox Berkeley, Hebrew songs by Ravel and Ury, and finally some folk songs of the United Nations from USA, Hungary, Poland, France, Canada and England.

Peter is a fabulous musician with wide knowledge of the singer's repertoire and he helped me greatly in preparation of recital programmes. He went with me to Geneva to give a recital in the Cours St Pierre in the Old Town where he received excellent critical notices for his part in the concert. Peter is a fine pianist and has worked as coach to a great many of today's young singers as well as the older generation. His work with Glyndebourne Chorus is legendary.

Another great coach and accompanist of German origin is Paul Hamburger with whom I worked a great deal. His understanding and knowledge of Lieder is vast and I was grateful for his help and encouragement in this field. He accompanied me for numerous broadcast recitals, as did those other fine accompanists of the past, Ernest Lush, Clifton Helliwell, Frederick Stone and Josephine Lee.

Strangely, I only gave two recitals with the legendary Gerald Moore. He was already at the top of the tree when I came on the scene and he was held in a certain amount of awe. He and Prof had been long-time friends and had given many concerts together. A lovely story that Prof used to tell concerned a recital that he and Gerald were giving at a music club. One of the songs was *Have you seen but a white lily grow*. The poem ends with the words 'Oh so white, so soft, so sweet is she' – repeated. Prof had one of those awful moments of complete blankness when he could not remember beyond 'Oh so white' – so he sang on, repeating these words over and over again. While taking a bow, he heard Gerald murmur 'What a brain!'

Another accompanist with whom I worked a lot was Nina Walker, who has had a fine career, working at Covent Garden for a time, and playing for many international artists. We got on splendidly – she was always warmly encouraging, supportive and knowledgeable. I invited her to play for me in a recital in Dubrovnik, Yugoslavia, which was part of the Dubrovnik Festival. It was high summer and very, very hot, so we made sure to arrive two days before the performance in order to acclimatise – a great luxury by today's standards. The recital took place in the courtyard of the Rector's Palace, a wonderful mediaeval building. The audience sat around the open central area, on the steps leading upwards and in a stone balcony which surrounded it. I found the heat exhausting but at least the concert was in the late evening so it was relatively cooler – though nerves always made one feel hot, whatever the outside temperature.

(It was a joy to return to Dubrovnik where Derrick and I had spent part of our honeymoon in September 1960. We had driven down through Italy, taking a boat over from Bari to Dubrovnik. There we were enchanted by this perfect mediaeval town, seemingly unchanged over the centuries. We found a room in a private house owned by a middle-aged couple who, pre-war, had been

With Nina Walker in the Rector's Palace, Dubrovnik

DUBROVAČKE LJETNE IGRE

SUMMER FESTIVAL - FESTIVAL D'ETE - SOMMERFESTSPIELE

ATRIJ KNEŽEVA DVORA — ATRIUM OF THE RECTOR'S PALACE

Sezona XVII — 1966. **1145** izvedba th performance

SRIJEDA, 10. VIII 1966. u 21 h Wednesday, 10 August at 9 p. m.

Solistički koncert - Recital

PAMELA BOWDEN

alt - London

NINA WALKER

klavir - London

Program:

G. F. Händel SWEETEST STILLNESS
Recitativ i arija iz oratorija „JEPHTA"

H. Purcell ALTIFIDORAN'S SONG

F. Schubert PET PJESAMA
Five Songs

B. Britten A CHARM OF LULLABIES

A. Hopkins (arr.) TRI FRANCUSKE NARODNE PJESME
French Folk Songs

CIJENE ULAZNICA OD 10.— DO 40.— N. DINARA

Ulaznice — Tickets — Billets — Karten:
Turistički informativni centar, tel. 23-54 / Atlas, tel. 20-23 / Narodno kazalište, tel. 22-38 od 8—12 i 17—19 h, na mjestu izvedbe od 20 h

Posjetiocima iz Kupara, Srebrenog, Mlina, Plata i Cavtata osiguran autobus za povratak
Posjetiocima iz Gruža i Lapad- - 'guran tramvaj za povratak

Spot the errors – the Dubrovnik handbill/programme

middle-class professionals. They were enduring considerable hardship and deprivation under the communist régime. We talked to them a lot during our brief stay and there was one delightful moment when, having seen my passport with its entry under occupation 'singer', they assumed that I was a sewing machine salesperson! Our friends' apartment was overlooking the wide main street of the town – a pedestrian precinct as no cars were permitted through the town gates. The town was surrounded by a high wall on to which one could climb at various points and stroll around the ramparts. The first evening we were surprised to hear a strange noise, a hissing, susurration, arising from below. Looking out of the window we beheld the nightly promenade of citizens strolling up and down the street – the noise was their feet on the stones polished to a smooth shine over the centuries. It was magical. It broke our hearts to hear that Dubrovnik had been shelled in 1991 during the Bosnian war, although I gather some of the damage was subsequently repaired.

The following year we went back for another holiday, this time to stay at an hotel along the coast. We drove down the coast road this time via Trieste, a journey that averaged about 25 miles per hour, since the road was as yet unmade, pitted with pot-holes and littered with large rocks to break the car's suspension. It wound along the coast, hanging on to the edge of mountains with the glorious sea dotted all the way with tiny islands. Occasionally we would pass road gangs tarmacking the surface – gangs is not quite the word. As Derrick put it, 'two men and a boy part-time'. Crossing the frontier into Yugoslavia was somewhat nerve-wracking because we had been foolish enough to load up the car with gifts for our friends, including a radio, which was an illegal possession, books, food and clothing. My heart was in my mouth as the grim Customs men searched the car, discovered the radio and books (all for our own use, honest, Guv.) and finally reluctantly decided we were OK tourists. I was never so pleased to cross a border – and not be slammed into a Slav jail for smuggling.)

AN ACCOMPANIST OF WHOM I don't have such happy memories was, nevertheless, a very celebrated partner of many well-known singers in the USA. He was the Hungarian Arpad Sandor who was based in New York. I met and worked with him on a recital programme when on a visit to New York in the late fifties. I was staying with the Fuller family. Frederick was at that time using his remarkable linguistic skills as an editor at the UN and they had a lovely apartment just off Fifth Avenue, not far from the Museum of Modern Art. Badly in need of a few days rest, I had opted to travel on a transatlantic liner from Southampton and I suppose it must have been among the last years that these great passenger liners were in regular service. It was a wonderfully restful outward voyage on the RMS Media from Liverpool,

Frederick Fuller and Heitor Villa-Lobos

with superb food and no-one to please but myself. It was a great thrill to stand on deck for our early morning arrival and to see the Statue of Liberty arising from the mist – I confess it brought a lump to my throat – on past Staten Island and into NY harbour with the hooters and sirens shouting their welcome. It sure beat landing in a jumbo at Kennedy Airport!

The stay was marked by highs and lows. Among the highs was the champagne atmosphere of the city, the museums, art galleries, stores like Macy's and Bloomingdales, and driving through the then quite perilous Central Park; there was a soirée at the home of one of the great American hostesses at which I was asked to sing a short recital of English songs and Lieder. Among the other guests performing was the guitarist Andrés Segovia. One Sunday afternoon we went to visit, at his apartment high above the park, the Brazilian composer Heitor Villa-Lobos. Our host spent the afternoon smoking villainous cigars, without which he was seldom seen, and occasionally adding to the music manuscript sheet in front of him. As he spoke no English and I no Portuguese, Frederick acted as interpreter. Villa-Lobos asked if I would learn and sing some of his songs – which would have been a great honour to do – and Frederick offered to teach me the Portuguese texts – but somehow, alas, we never managed to sort out the songs and it was a sadly missed opportunity.

Among the lows of the trip could be counted a failure to 'gell' musically with Arpad. I found him opinionated and inflexible, and our musical ideas never happily coincided. The other low point was entirely my own fault and due to naiveté. One lunchtime some friends and I went to a bar for an aperitif after a shopping spree. I ordered a dry martini. The barman asked 'How dry, ma'am?' and I answered 'Very dry' meaning, to me, a dry not sweet Martini. I since learned that his interpretation was a glass full of gin at which he waved the Martini bottle, duly shaken and ice-cold. It was delicious but lethal and after a second one, it was not until we emerged into the sunlight that I realised quite how lethal. I was due to sing that evening to the distinguished players of the Bach Aria Group with the prospect of becoming one of their regular solo singers. Despite a sleep, a meal and some frantic practising, the alcohol had roughened the voice so that I sang well below my best and, in short, messed up. Needless to say I was not asked to sing with them again, which was a great pity because their repertoire of Bach and baroque was exactly what suited me and which I loved. It taught me a lesson and thereafter I never drank spirits within 48 hours of singing. A glass of wine or sherry was harmless but spirits were a no-no.

The voyage back on the liner United States was marked by meeting someone who became a lifelong family friend, Lord Geddes, who was then chairman of the merchant fleet division of P&O. I visited their home in Scotland and became friendly with their daughter Margaret. She and I became pregnant with our first children at the same time and Ross Geddes became my daughter's godfather.

THE SOLO PIANISTS whom I met made equally strong impressions – there was the diminutive Shura Cherkassky to whom I was introduced at a dinner party at Emmie Tillett's home. He was a humorous and lively conversationalist, bubbling over with fun.

For a few years there existed a club for musicians in South Audley Street in London's West End, called the MM Club – standing for Mainly Musicians.

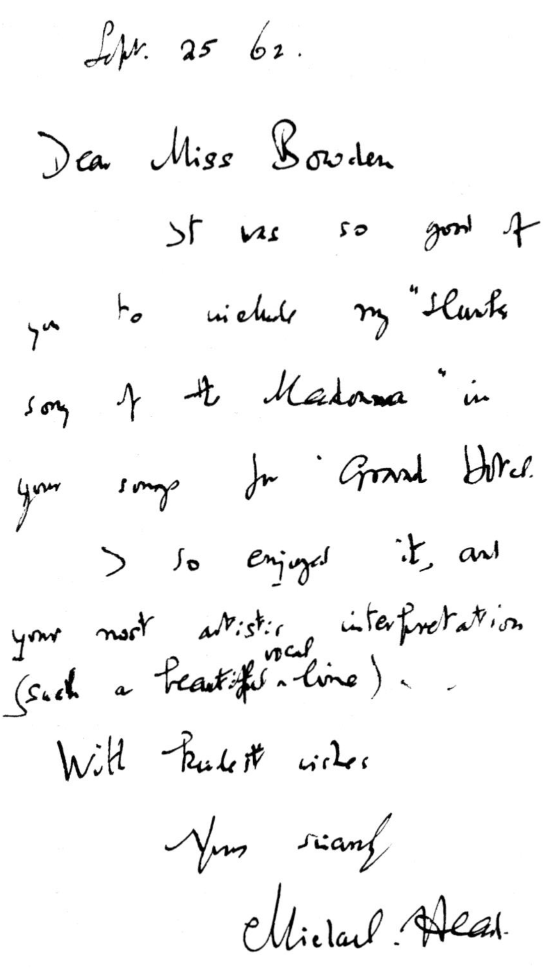
Sept. 25 62.

Dear Miss Bowden

It was so good of you to include my "Slumber Song of the Madonna" in your songs for 'Grand Hotel.'

I so enjoyed it, and your most artistic interpretation (such a beautiful vocal line)..

With kindest wishes

Yours sincerely

Michael Head.

A quick but nonetheless highly appreciated note from Michael Head

It was an elegant house furnished with beautiful antiques and it was there that my parents took Prof and Mrs Prof to dinner after my return from Geneva in 1954 to thank them for all they had done to help me so far.

It was also at the MM Club that I first met the pianist Denis Matthews. He was by then internationally famous as a great Mozart and Beethoven interpreter and it was a thrill to meet him. He had a fine intellect and prolific memory; he was able to sit at the piano and play huge chunks of Wagner operas, creating orchestral textures and colours, only stopping to enthuse:

'Just listen to that – see what he has done here – what amazing modulations', and so on. He tried hard to enthuse me for Wagner but without great success as I have always found his music overheated and excessive in both density and length.

At that time Denis was President of the Henley-on-Thames Music Society – he lived in a lovely house in Henley with his wife Mira and family. He invited me to give a recital in the Henley Subscription Concerts series in Henley Town Hall and offered to accompany me. I was naturally excited at the thought of performing with such a famous pianist and we set about choosing the programme of Handel, Purcell, Schubert, Brahms, Berkeley and Hopkins. This was so successful that we planned another recital together two years later. Feeling that we ought to include a work which would display his mastery of the piano, we decided on *Seven Popular Spanish Songs* by de Falla as one of the groups of songs.

Rehearsals were a joy and we both found great pleasure in working on achieving an accord in the interpretations of the programme. I hadn't reckoned with the temperament of the soloist, however! When it came to the concert, the first half went quite well but the de Falla songs went almost out of control. Denis enjoyed himself so much with the showy, exotic accompaniments that our carefully prepared tempi, pauses, breathing places and detailed phrasing were somewhat modified!

THERE WERE MANY contemporary composers whose works I was privileged to sing over the years and I was lucky enough to get to know several of them. I speak elsewhere of Vaughan Williams and Britten, two giants of the twentieth century, and of Sir Arthur Bliss and John McCabe. Another who was greatly admired was Sir Lennox Berkeley, and I was thrilled to be asked to record his *Four Poems of St Teresa of Avila* with orchestra conducted by John Minchinton. This proved to be my all-time favourite disc – the songs were ideal for my voice and I found them both beautifully written and profoundly moving. Sir Michael Tippett was another great favourite and I took part in the first recording of his wonderful oratorio *A Child of Our Time* conducted by John Pritchard with the Royal Liverpool Philharmonic Orchestra and chorus, and with as fellow soloists the delightful Elsie Morison (later to become Mrs Rafael Kubelik), Richard Lewis and Richard Standen, all of whom sang with great commitment and beauty of tone. With Michael conducting, we also did some concerts together, programming *Sosostris's Aria* from his opera *A Midsummer Marriage* with the Scottish National Orchestra.

Through mutual friends I got to know Malcolm Arnold well and sang in a few concerts with him as conductor – we used string orchestra arrangements of songs by Purcell and the Berkeley songs in the programmes. My delight was considerable when he offered to write a set of songs especially for me – he chose poems by William Blake and the settings were sensitive and atmospheric, with lyrical orchestration. We did several broadcasts of the songs as well as concert performances but not a commercial recording. Many years later we met again and regretted the fact that no recording existed. My amazement can be imagined when, in 1997, the BBC contacted me to say that they were bringing out a CD in celebration of Sir Malcolm's 75th birthday and would I agree to our recording of the *Five William Blake Songs* being included! It turned out that they had kept a performance broadcast from Manchester with the BBC Philharmonic Orchestra and it was mercifully free of coughs and audience noise. It was also a very satisfactory performance so we were extremely happy.

There was once a brief meeting with Shostakovitch. He attended a Prom at the Albert Hall and came around to the Green Room after the concert. My impression was of a small, shy man with round pebble glasses, wearing a rather shabby mac. As he spoke no English and I no Russian, our meeting consisted of smiles and nods, and a murmur from his interpreter.

There were of course a number of other composers whose works I sang. For example there was Edwin Roxburgh with his fine *Recitative after Blake* and Christopher Brown with his oratorio *David* of which we gave the first performance at the Three Choirs Festival. There was also Stephen Dodgson who wrote a superb piece for me entitled *Epigrams from a Garden* for contralto and clarinet choir of which we gave the first performance at the Harrogate Festival in 1977 with Harry Legge conducting.

I must mention a special lady whose settings of English poetry are of the highest quality. Elaine Hugh-Jones, who was a well-known professional accompanist, has written many splendid songs to poems by R S Thomas and Keats, among others. These are distinguished not only by exciting, colourful and singable vocal lines but also by complex accompaniments of much interest to complement the melodies. I have performed her songs in concert and on radio, and have recommended advanced students to take them into their repertoires.

Act II, Scene 9
Glyndebourne Again

IT WAS IN 1967 that my agent, Emmie Tillett, rang one day to say that Glyndebourne had asked if I would be interested in singing the role of Madame Larina in their next season's new production of Tchaikowsky's *Yevgeny Onegin*. It would be the first time the opera has been given there and it would be sung in Russian. There would be 15 performances plus a broadcast. Was I interested! The money was, as one expected, minimal, but I was happy at the thought of going back to Glyndebourne in such a pleasant role. Since the chorus days I had been back, in 1966, to sing a few performances as Second Witch in *Dido and Aeneas* but that was all. I had, however, been honoured to take part in John Christie's memorial service in Westminster Abbey on 3 September 1962. Vittorio Gui conducted a performance of Mozart's *Requiem* with Elsie Morison, Richard Lewis, Carlo Cava and myself as soloists, with the Glyndebourne Festival Chorus and the Royal Philharmonic Orchestra. It was a moving occasion, bringing to an end the first era of the Glyndebourne Festival Opera.

Already mentioned is the television production of *Onegin* some years earlier. This was conducted by David Lloyd-Jones and directed by Basil Coleman. It was just as colour TV was coming in but alas ours was filmed in black and white. It was also before domestic video recorders so I never had a copy to keep and it must have been deleted or thrown away by now. Basil was a sensitive director with whom I enjoyed working – we had already met at Aldeburgh. In the opening scene, Larina is thinking nostalgically about her girlhood and in a close-up Basil asked me to have a far-away look. The right expression was achieved by unfocussing the eyes and he said yes, that's just what we want. As is usual in TV opera, one didn't get an overall impression of the performance while taking part – there was no sense of a stage, only small sets, and of course the orchestra was in another studio. We heard and watched monitors for our cues. David as conductor had a fine understanding of the style and was steeped in the Russian tradition, speaking the language fluently.

George Christie's letter of thanks
after the Mozart Requiem, sung for his father in Westminster Abbey

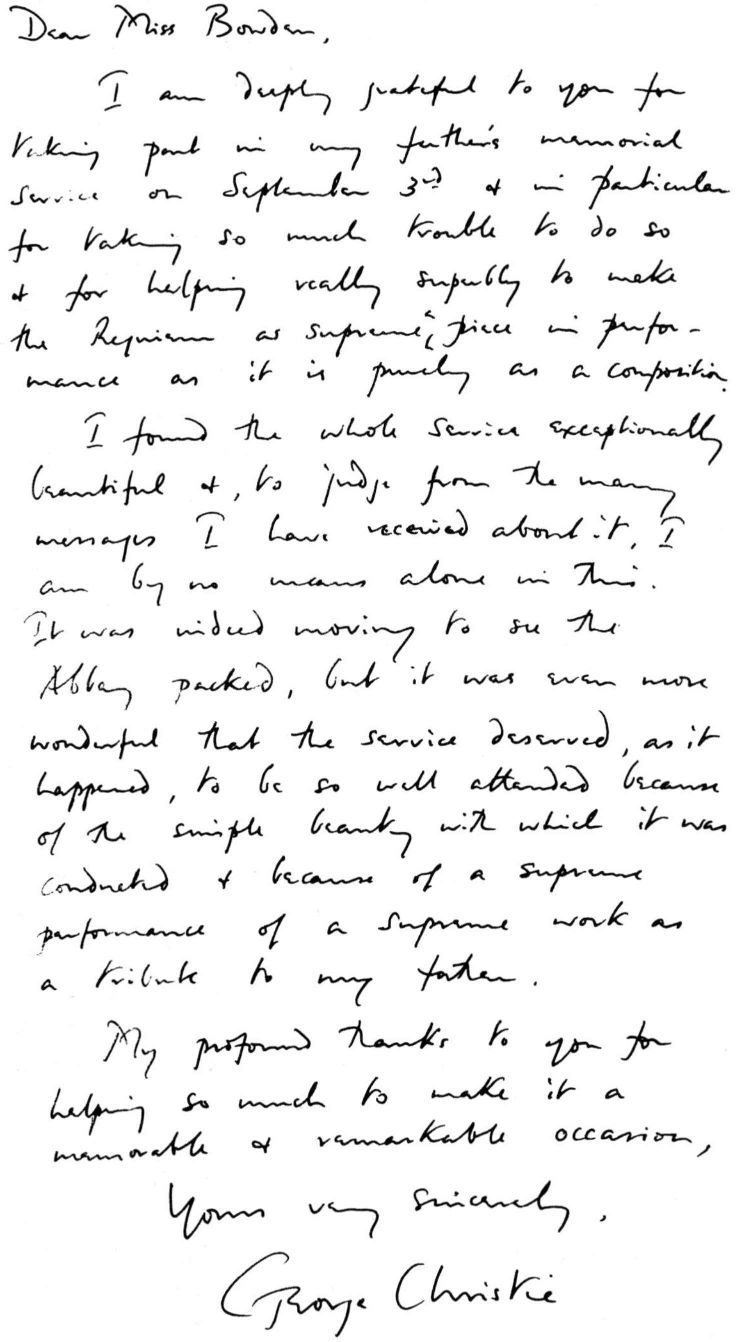

Dear Miss Bowden,

I am deeply grateful to you for taking part in my father's memorial service on September 3rd & in particular for taking so much trouble to do so & for helping really superbly to make the Requiem as supreme a piece in performance as it is purely as a composition.

I found the whole service exceptionally beautiful &, to judge from the many messages I have received about it, I am by no means alone in this. It was indeed moving to see the Abbey packed, but it was even more wonderful that the service deserved, as it happened, to be so well attended because of the simple beauty with which it was conducted & because of a supreme performance of a supreme work as a tribute to my father.

My profound thanks to you for helping so much to make it a memorable & remarkable occasion,

Yours very sincerely,

George Christie

In order to prepare for the Glyndebourne production, I took a course in Russian at a language school and went again to the great dramatic soprano Oda Slobodskaya for some coaching. The school was of limited use but the hours spent with Mme Slobodskaya (or Slobbie) were magical. She would sit at the piano pounding out the vocal part and shouting the words in her huge voice. She had been such a help previously with the text of *Kontchakovna's Cavatina* from Prince Igor that I had faith that she would tutor me well once again.

Nevertheless one felt very shy and nervous when it came to the first run-through with the rest of the cast in the Organ Room one sunny afternoon in May 1968. Apart from Hugues Cuenod who sang the role of Monsieur Triquet (in French) and Elizabeth Söderström (Tatyana) they were all from eastern Europe and more-or-less native Russian speakers. They were encouraging, much to my relief, and said my accent was 'very high class'!!

That summer was idyllic. Our director, Michael Hadjimischchev, had a penetrating understanding of the Pushkin story and the atmosphere of 19th century Russia, with its landed gentry, peasantry and social life of St Petersburg. He was able to direct us in exactly how our characters would have behaved, the etiquette and mores of the time. His father had been a diplomat and Michael was widely travelled and cultured. The conductor was John Pritchard, an old friend from the chorus days when he was chorus master, and later in many concerts, including our recording of Tippett's *A Child of Our Time*. He allowed the music to breathe and brought out the romantic yet disciplined warmth of the score.

The Bulgarian mezzo Virginia Popova, who sang the role of the nurse, became, and remains, one of my dearest friends though we have been unable to see each other often. She had to be very careful what she said about conditions in her home town Sofia because there were Communist 'minders' hovering around the edge of her life, but she had clearly had a difficult, even deprived, existence – even though she was one of the principal singers in the Sofia Opera. That first year her husband was unable to come to England with her, although he was allowed out for a short visit the following season.

Another singer whom I admired enormously was the fine soprano Elizabeth Söderström. Her Russian was perfect since her mother came from Russia and she sang the leading role of Tatyana most beautifully. She was a generous colleague who never stepped out of the role on stage and gave everything when one was singing with her in a scene. We found great sympathy between us as mother and daughter.

As Madame Larina in Yevgeny Onegin, Glyndebourne, 1968

In real life I was also the mother – our baby son Justin was only four months old when we started rehearsals so we rented a small house in Lewes where Justin and his nanny stayed with me while daughter Michèle, then just five years old, stayed in London with the au pair and my husband, coming down to Lewes for weekends. The little house bulged at the seams and luckily our very capable young nanny managed to get Justin to sleep through the night, so we had reasonably undisturbed sleep. Justin, however, did disturb the peace in the opera house, not in that season but in the following one two years later. His nanny took him in to a rehearsal one afternoon and he sat transfixed until I had to leave the stage. From the stalls came an agonised cry, 'Come back, Mummy!' which was all the more audible throughout the building as he managed to yell right into the producer's microphone!

The performances of *Onegin* were very well received by the critics and there were some gratifying comments about my own part. By now the regime had changed and George Christie, with his wife Mary, was in charge. They carried on the tradition of the strawberries and cream teas and the various parties. Other operas came into rehearsal and then performance, with many friends coming down to take part.

At one performance early in the season I managed to get seats for Slobbie on the very front row of the stalls. At the end, when we were all taking curtains, she was to be seen applauding enthusiastically while jabbing her finger towards us with cries of 'Bravo YOU, bravo YOU'. No, it wasn't me she was pointing to but our excellent tenor Wieslaw Ochman who sang the role of Lensky. There's gratitude, I thought.

Madame Larina became the only operatic role that I sang many times. In the end it lasted for three full Glyndebourne seasons, 1968, 1970 and 1975, with also the tour in 1969 when we took the production to Manchester, Leeds, Liverpool, Newcastle and Nottingham. We also sang a semi-staged performance at a Prom in 1970 at the end of the season – one of the first operas to be given in a Prom season.

It was my proud boast that nobody else had sung the role at Glyndebourne until *Onegin* was given again at the opening of the newly-built opera house in 1994 – by which time I had been long retired from singing. (The production was, *of course*, not a patch on ours).

In his book on the history of Glyndebourne, Spike Hughes wrote something completely fanciful. After mentioning the decision to perform in the original language and comments about the superb performance of Elizabeth Söderström and those of other singers in the cast, he said, 'The two neatest performances, however, came from singers with no Slav blood in them. Hugues Cuenod's brilliant little study of Monsieur Triquet, the French tutor, was one; the other was the Larina of Pamela Bowden, whose agent recommended her for an entirely novel qualification – namely, that she had a Russian au pair girl.' Where on earth he got that little gem from I'll never know – needless to say I never did have a Russian au pair girl and hardly think Mme Slobodskaya fitted that description!

(On the subject of au pair girls, we counted ourselves very fortunate in that of the variety of nationalities and personalities who came to us when the children were small, two in particular have become the closest of friends. There was Juliette Chapuis, a beautiful diminutive French girl of Vietnamese background who settled in Tours with her husband and two sons, and we see each other from time to time – their eldest son, Fabrice, is a great friend of Justin's. And then there was Christa Kraft who became almost our adopted daughter, a wonderful, warm, generous person and opera lover. She married, settled in Klagenfurt, Austria, and had twin sons and a daughter. Christa is Justin's godmother and we exchange visits frequently when not on the phone or e-mail. Finally there was our nanny, Susan Bullock, a Lancashire lass from Wigan, who eased my life by keeping her charges happy and healthy with a vast variety of nanny-type tricks, treats and skills.)

In 1971 I was approached by the Royal Opera to sing in their new production of *Onegin* and to take the role of the nurse. I suggested that while I would be willing to do so, wouldn't they prefer that I sing my accustomed role of Larina. They asked me to go along and sing for Sir Georg Solti who was to conduct, and as a result I was engaged for seven performances.

This was a very different experience from Glyndebourne. Tatyana was sung this time by Ileana Cotrubas, Lensky by Robert Tear and Prince Gremin by Don Garrard. The director was Peter Hall who came to the work for the first time and did not have the same feeling for the period nor the same sensitivity for detail to which we had been accustomed. This production showed an altogether cruder country family and my role was given much less interest. It was also musically taut and nervy. To make matters worse, I hated my costume – it was so padded as to make me look very fat and dumpy, and the wig was horrible, just the wrong shape altogether.

That wig caused me great embarrassment at the reception after the first night. It was a gala performance in the presence of the Queen Mother and we were bidden to be received by her at a reception to which we had to go immediately after the final curtain still in costume. When it came to my turn to curtsey and shake hands, I found to my horror that I couldn't hear a word Her Majesty said to me. I could see her lips moving but not a sound penetrated the curtains of the beastly wig over my ears. I can only hope that my smiles and nods and Yes, Ma'ams made some kind of sense.

Act II, Scene 10
Retirement?

I HAD MADE UP MY MIND early in my career that I would retire at the first sign of vocal ageing, and that I would not wait until people said 'Why doesn't she give it up?' It seemed that many singers begin to show signs of wear after the age of 50, the quality of tone may become thinner, unsteadiness and wide vibrato may develop and breath shortens. Against this one can counter with long-standing technique and above all, artistic maturity and interpretative experience. It is a sad fact that by the time one has learnt as much as one can and accumulated years of knowledge and understanding of what makes a fine singer, nature robs one of the very means to continue to share all that with the public.

There has been research over the past three decades into the ageing voice, and knowing what we now know, perhaps retirement from the platform could have been delayed for at least another five years. As it was, I began to feel some weakness in part of my voice and asked my husband – always an honest critic – to come to a performance of *Messiah* and tell me what he thought. He said that he could not hear a dramatic change but did admit that perhaps there was the beginning of loss of strength. No more needed to be said – I decided to cease to accept engagements. My last *Messiah* took place on Good Friday, 8 April 1977, at The Dome, Brighton, and my last public performance was Tippett's great oratorio *A Child of Our Time*, at the cathedral of Bury St Edmunds in Suffolk, conducted by an old friend, Harrison Oxley, in December 1979. The last broadcast was a concert performance of Handel's *Semele* in the role of Ino, at St John's Smith Square before an invited audience.

It must be confessed that there was a certain relief at the prospect of no more anxiety about colds and infections, no more packing evening dresses, no more scheduled planes and trains or long drives – it was as if a weight was lifted from my shoulders. Not until much later did I truly miss the thrill of walking on stage or platform to take part in the music I so loved. It has never in all these years since, though, ceased to feel odd to sit in an auditorium as one of the audience; my true place is still up there on the platform.

Act III, Scene 1

The Incorporated Society of Musicians

THE INCORPORATED SOCIETY OF MUSICIANS is the UK's professional body for all musicians, whether performers, composers, teachers, lecturers, therapists or musicologists. It provides complete professional support for musicians on an individual basis throughout their careers, and supplies a multitude of services, also with representation of their interests in all relevant situations.

Since joining the ISM in 1957 I had taken an active part in its affairs, serving on the committee of the Solo Performers' Section, as it was then called, and becoming its Warden in 1970. Later I was asked to be on the Council and then the Executive Committee, on which I was sitting in 1975. A new General Secretary, Susan Alcock, had just been appointed and she had plans to increase the Head Office staff by appointing an Assistant Administrator with responsibility for the Solo Performers' Section. Part of the job was to run the Young Artists' Recitals with which I had been connected as a member of the audition panel. A series of Wigmore Hall recitals was promoted by the ISM for selected artists chosen at audition, and had proved an attraction to bring young members into the Society. I knew that I had a flair for organisation which had hitherto been underused – though the family never forgot our small daughter running to her father one day to complain, 'Daddy, Mummy's organamising (*sic*) us again'!

My application for the post was greeted at first with incredulity – did I really mean it? Could I really give up my singing career already? The answers to these questions were affirmative and the President of the year, Richard Lewis, and other officers of the ISM welcomed me with enthusiasm. I insisted that I must be able to remain a member of the ISM as well as being an employee. Also it was agreed that I should honour remaining concert engagements and have time for some teaching.

So started a nine-year period that became the second large portion of my working life. There was much to do – the ISM was fast changing, we moved offices from the rather dreary premises in Gloucester Place to the third floor of the Royal Society of Musicians' beautiful house in Stratford Place off Oxford Street. It was a huge undertaking and in the process some fascinating archives were unearthed from a dusty, damp basement, containing records of the Society's business and the great musical names associated with it since its inception in 1883.

For the most part I greatly enjoyed the work, and the most enjoyable was when I was in contact with new young artists and arranging the details of the auditions, the recitals, publicity, and so on. I learnt an enormous amount about administration and had great support from fellow administrator Elizabeth Poulsen, in charge of the Private Teachers' and the Music in Education Sections, and the Deputy General Secretary Walter Jeffrey. When Walter left to become General Secretary of the Writers' Guild, my office lost a lot of fun and laughs. Sadly, he died tragically young in 1991. He was a

An ISM audition panel for Young Artists recitals: (back) John Russell, Derek Hammond-Stroud, Marjorie Thomas; (front) Susan Alcock (ISM General Secretary), Gordon Greene, myself, John McCabe, Alan Harverson, Ralph Downes

With Ian Wallace at an ISM party, Kenwood

great joker and never allowed me to forget an occasion that happened during the year of office as President of Lady Barbirolli. There was to be an event held at the School of Pharmacy of London University, and Walter and I went over to make some advance preparations. We were greeted by the head porter who knew that Evelyn Barbirolli was expected to arrive. When I was out of earshot he said to Walter, pointing to me, 'Of course, that's Lady Barbirolli, inn'it? Yer can always tell a lady, she stands out in a crowd.' For ever afterwards, Walter would whisper, when we were in public, 'Remember, you stand out in a crowd.'

In time, we were obliged to give up the Young Artists' Recitals due to the escalating costs of mounting the recitals and also the proliferation of competitions for young artists both nationally and internationally. I felt that we still needed to be doing more to help performers in general and came up with the idea of putting on concerts in different parts of the country to promote musicians of up to age 40 who had never been able to take advantage of competitions due to a later than usual start or a change in direction. We needed to find funding for such a scheme, so I set about trying to get the interest of a sponsor. Luckily it did not take long before striking lucky and persuading National Westminster Bank to fund the project. They were ideal sponsors, taking a personal interest but never interfering or attaching strings to their generosity. Thus was born the ISM/NatWest Festival Days scheme.

In the first year, we were able to take small groups of artists to three separate towns such as Derby, Nottingham, Liverpool, etc. where we hired suitable concert halls, publicised the events and personally invited concert agents, impresarios, secretaries of music societies of all kinds, in fact anyone who might offer engagements. I gave interviews for local radio stations and we did everything we could to promote the artists. Again, they were selected by audition and we had to put together panels of experts in every discipline from singers to pianists, string players, wind and brass players – even organists wanted to be heard. NatWest offered us an initial three-year term that they eventually extended to five years. After that, we reluctantly had to end the scheme, though the number of artists who went on to make excellent careers was gratifying.

LIFE AT THE ISM was always interesting – I enjoyed keeping in contact with all the musician friends from past years and making new ones – meeting people I had not come across as a singer; solo instrumentalists, well-known teachers and music educationalists.

There were, of course, some down-sides. Particularly unenjoyable was the role of negotiator, and at that time there were sticky relationships with the unions. I was obliged to be part of the team at many meetings with the Musicians' Union and with Equity, trying to establish good working relationships and sorting out differences. I also became responsible for negotiating the annual update of minimum fee recommendations with the BBC for both radio and TV contracts. It was not really a world in which I felt comfortable but fortunately it was only a small part of the overall work.

Act III, Scene 2
The London College of Music

IN 1985 I WAS APPROACHED by the composer and pianist John McCabe who had just been appointed Director of the London College of Music, succeeding Dr William Lloyd Webber (father of Andrew and Julian).

John said he was looking for someone to head the singing department, and would I be interested. By now I was feeling the need to surround myself again with music-making, and had been doing enough teaching privately to have become fascinated by the process of training singers.

I said that it would indeed be interesting, providing that I could have a free rein in completely reorganising the department and creating a structured three-year course, introducing many new classes. John immediately agreed and I duly handed in my resignation to the ISM and started the next phase of my life in September 1986. I thought I would give it five years to see how things developed. Little did I think this phase would last for thirteen years and see very many ups and downs.

In preparation I set down what I considered essential for singing students and then formed it into a workable timetable. As well as their weekly voice lesson, there were to be classes in opera, oratorio, movement, repertoire, languages (Italian, German and French), second-study piano, and a series of workshops and master classes by visiting teachers. With complete support from John McCabe – despite the considerable additional cost – we were able to put the new regime in place immediately. The students were shell-shocked, moving from virtually no classes to a very full timetable.

Already teaching there were the Australian soprano Janice Chapman, and the tenor Laurence Watts. I invited Soo Bee Lee to join us and we became the core vocal faculty, together with Michael Goldthorpe, Henry Herford joining us for a while and also Peter Savidge until pressure of concert engagements compelled them to leave. Later on Eileen Price, who had been Head of Singing at the Welsh College of Music and Drama, and Gordon Stewart joined us, both becoming towers of strength. More recently Therees Hibbard came to work with mainly Music Theatre students, carrying on the work of Mary Hammond. In our early days at Great Marlborough Street I had invited Mary to give classes in Music Theatre, the first conservatoire to offer this subject. Mary directed a number of very successful excerpts and we collaborated on presentations of Menotti's *Amahl and the Night Visitors*. This was extremely valuable experience for the students, who were able to learn new vocal skills, including ways of creating a Music Theatre sound, required by directors of musicals, without danger to the voice. Mary later left us, with mutual regret, to inaugurate a Music Theatre course, now well-established, at the Royal Academy of Music. Other conservatoires have followed suit.

The building in Great Marlborough Street that was our home had a listed façade but the inside showed signs of age. It was not very big and probably because of this, the students liked the friendliness of our small college. We did have a pleasant concert hall, which was eventually given a glamorous face-life, in which we gave many concerts, with choral and orchestral concerts at other venues. We even managed to mount small opera productions, such as *Dido and Aeneas*, Gluck's *Orfeo* (which I conducted), Menotti's *Amahl and the Night Visitors* and scenes from some of the Mozart operas. For bigger productions we had to go elsewhere and one very successful opera was Handel's *Orlando* which we put on at the beautiful St Cyprian's Church near Baker Street. In 1986 I had the idea of putting on a mini-festival of singing and decided to call it simply 'Singing Week'. There were two events each day, a lunch-time recital or lecture and an evening performance. We invited guest speakers, teachers and performers covering as wide a range as possible of vocal styles, techniques and skills.

We were able to raise money from sponsors to finance the week, which was a huge success and put our vocal department firmly on the map. The next year the piano faculty under Raphael Terroni followed suit with a Piano Week.

It was early in 1990 that I was approached by Carola Grindea, Chairman of ISSTIP (International Society for the Study of Tension in Performance) with her idea for the establishment of a clinic to help musicians suffering from related stress injuries, to include singers with vocal stress problems, and also psychological difficulties. It was to be freely available to all music students and we would work together, with the added involvement of a number of medical consultants, regularly Dr C Wynn Parry, who was extremely interested in the project and already a founder member of BAPAM (British Association of Performing Arts Medicine).

LONDON COLLEGE OF MUSIC
SINGING WEEK: 3 – 7 NOVEMBER 1986
Programme of Events

MONDAY 3 NOVEMBER:

1.00 – 2.00 pm	Recital: Peter Savidge, baritone David Owen Norris, piano
7.00 – 9.00 pm	Composer & Interpreter. Dr Malcolm Williamson

TUESDAY 4 NOVEMBER:

12.30 – 2.00 pm	Opera – illustrated talk. Elsa Mayer-Lisman
7.00 – 9.00 pm	The Art of Accompanying. Nina Walker

WEDNESDAY 5 NOVEMBER:

1.00 – 2.00 pm	'But what does it mean?' Talk about words. David Lennox
7.00 – 9.00 pm	Opera Workshop. Douglas Craig

THURSDAY 6 NOVEMBER:

12.30 – 2.00 pm	Performing early music. Andrew Parrott
7.00 – 9.00 pm	Teaching choir training. Norman Tattersall

FRIDAY 7 NOVEMBER:

12.30 – 2.00 pm	Performing contemporary music. Gregory Rose
7.00 – 9.00 pm	Master Class. John Carol Case

We therefore, with the permission of the Director, set up a weekly clinic at the LCM which was opened in April 1990. From the start it attracted students and professional musicians with problems from London colleges, orchestras, and from all over the country. Thanks to a huge amount of work and dedication from Carola, the clinic is still going strong twelve years later, and we now run a course to train teachers in the various principles involved.

We organise a big seminar nearly every year, recently at the Royal Festival Hall, and the number of 'patients' seen and helped now runs into several hundreds.

We have our own website on the internet and there is a lot of interest from other countries where ISSTIP has branches. Our guiding principle is 'Prevention is better than cure'; and we try to give guidance in postural problems, overcoming stage fright, the psychological approach to performing, and so on, with valuable help from many specialists such as the now very famous Dr Mosaref Ali, Barry Green, author of *The Inner Game of Music*, Tom Harris, otolaryngologist, and many others.

Our small faculty gathered strength at Great Marlborough Street but sadly the LCM Council under the inspired chairmanship of Clive Marks, of which I had become a member, had to make a decision about the future. The finances were rocky and it was clear that we could not maintain our private status, unfunded by government and totally reliant upon student fees for income. We looked around for new premises and an established educational body with which to co-operate. We eventually found an enthusiastic ally in the principal of the then Ealing College of Higher Education who was keen to provide a home for the LCM at their modern premises in St Mary's Road, Ealing. He and his college were prepared to create studios, teaching rooms and offices, and plans were laid. As was to be expected, there was opposition to the move from some students and staff, and for a time a cloud of dissension and antagonism hung over our previously happy community. Disaster and the demise of the LCM were foretold. However, those of us involved made sure that the terms of the agreement were such that the LCM was assured of its independent existence and the continuation of its name in the new alliance, though financial control was to be in the hands of the Ealing College – and so it worked out.

We were all sad to leave the old building and the move took place in the summer of 1990. This was not without its crises, one of which was when a grand piano being crane-lifted out of the top floor windows fell with a crash on to the pavement of Great Marlborough Street, most luckily missing our Registrar, John Chapman, by a whisker.

It took us some months to settle in to our new quarters and perhaps the most disturbing aspect was the fact that we no longer had a focus, our rooms being dispersed, and there was no separate LCM staff or student rooms in which to be together. There was a rather grand staff room, furnished with leather button-back chesterfields and a bar, for all the Ealing staff and we gradually began to feel at home there.

In the interim between the agreement being signed and our move, the College of Higher Education was raised to University status and became Thames Valley University. As a separate unit we kept our own external examination system, and diplomas for graduates remained the same for a while but later, as eventually happened in all music conservatories the university awarded a B.Mus degree as the final examination. We continued to mount opera and music theatre productions such as Menotti's *The Telephone* in double bill with Malcolm Williamson's *The Happy Prince*, Gilbert and Sullivan's *The Mikado*, Howard Goodall's *Silas Marner*, Puccini's *Suor Angelica*, Weill's *Mahagonny Songspiel*, and again *Dido and Aeneas* and excerpts from *The Marriage of Figaro* plus many music theatre shows. We were keenly supported by Malcolm Williamson himself and by Howard Goodall, who became closely associated with the LCM and was always willing to take time from his busy schedule to take a class with my students.

We also continued to invite well-known singers to give masterclasses and workshops – the excellent tenor Ryland Davies and the clever, and very funny, singer and composer Betty Roe gave us great support, among many others, including a number of our American colleagues who were always generously willing to visit us when over here.

Much has changed over the past ten years; there were comings and goings at the top; structures changed and after John McCabe's departure at the time of the move, new directors came and went, with different titles and duties.

Through it all, despite the prophets of doom, the LCM has survived, albeit vastly changed, in some ways for the better and some the opposite. I tried to preserve our integrity in the singing department and was able to keep the structure that had been built up in place for quite a few years. Things change and move on – we had to accept cuts and adaptations but still tried to maintain the high standards we had always aspired to for our singers. We still put on two stage performances a year, there was still a major choral concert every year, and many lunch-time recitals, masterclasses, visiting teachers and so on.

For reasons of the overall policy of the College, however, we were forced to adapt to an ethos that did not sit happily with me. Perhaps it was too late for me to change! I finally decided to resign as Head of Vocal Studies in 1998. My successor, whom I strongly supported as a candidate, is the excellent baritone Peter Savidge. We have worked closely together to make the handover seamless and he is now firmly installed. I still teach an occasional student, just to keep an eye on them all!

Act IV, Scene 1

Competitions, Conferences, Committees and things

QUITE APART FROM THE MAIN THRUST of my LCM teaching there have been other important strands in my professional life. The first college where I was invited to teach was the Colchester Institute, where my old friend Norman Tattersall was Head of Singing. He invited me firstly to judge a prize that he had instituted in honour of the great Wagnerian Eva Turner who had recently died – she had been greatly loved. She would preside regally at many musical gatherings and was a sought-after teacher. Then, after taking a monthly class at Colchester, I agreed to teach on a more regular basis and accepted a few advanced students. Eventually these became weekly visits but the journeys became too much and I decided to leave, but not before taking on the task of directing the Opera Class in Vaughan Williams' *Sir John in Love.*

(My choice of this opera arose from a broadcast concert performance of it in which I had sung the role of Mistress Quickly during 'Uncle Ralph's' lifetime. I remember sitting at his feet at a post-performance party at his home and swearing to remember every word he spoke. I didn't immediately write it down and so, of course, cannot now bring back a word. He was very deaf by this time and had a curious trumpet hearing aid which he called his 'teapot'.

Soon after the death of Vaughan Williams it was a great privilege to be asked to give the first broadcast performance of his touching, emotive *Four Last Songs*. The poems were by Ursula Vaughan Williams, and she gave me some valuable insights into their conception. This was a work that always reduced me to tears in rehearsal at home, and I could only perform it by metaphorically standing to one side and forgetting the personal reaction in the interests of communication – which, as a professional, one must.)

FROM TIME TO TIME I have given master classes at Birmingham Conservatoire where Keith Darlington was a highly effective and charming Head of Singing. Their modern building in the centre of Birmingham was

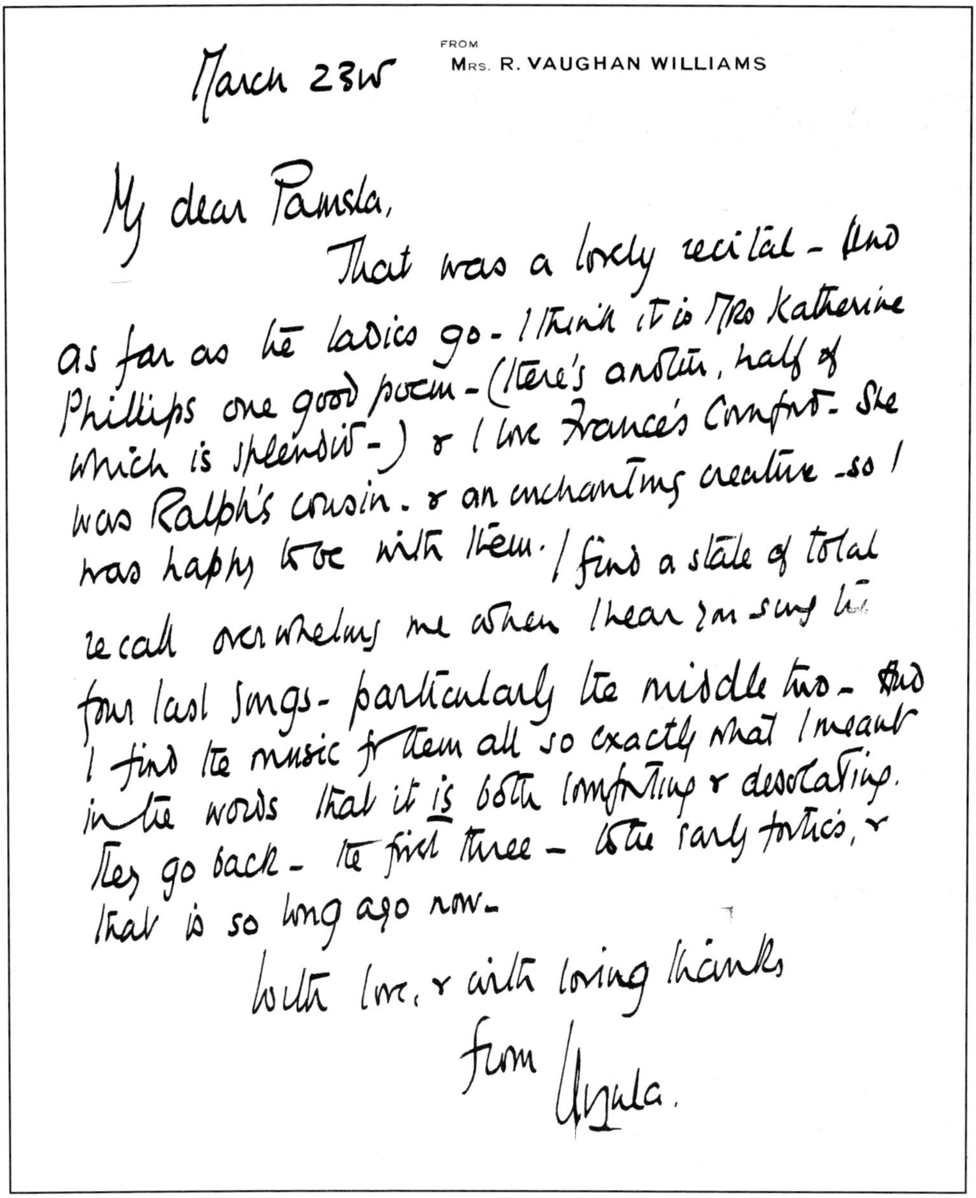

FROM
MRS. R. VAUGHAN WILLIAMS

March 23rd

My dear Pamela,

That was a lovely recital – and as far as the ladies go – I think it is Mrs Katherine Phillips one good poem – (there's another, half of which is splendid –) & I love Frances's Comfort – she was Ralph's cousin. & an enchanting creature – so I was happy to be with them. I find a state of total recall overwhelming me when I hear you sing the four last songs – particularly the middle two – and I find the music for them all so exactly what I meant in the words that it *is* both comforting & desolating. They go back – the first three – to the early forties, & that is so long ago now –

With love, & with loving thanks

from

Ursula.

From Ursula Vaughan Williams, about his Four Last Songs

a source of envy in contrast with our old LCM premises! Keith too invited me to teach there regularly but again I refused because of the awkward and tiring journey.

There is no doubt that I could be accused of inconsistency when, soon afterwards, I accepted an invitation from Gordon Stewart, newly appointed Head of Vocal Studies and Opera at the Royal Scottish Academy of Music and Drama in Glasgow. Gordon had been a Senior Music Producer at the BBC prior to this appointment. He has an encyclopaedic knowledge of the vocal repertoire and is an experienced accompanist. I had already been a regular visitor to Glasgow in David Kelly's time as Head of Singing, as an examiner for the end-of-year exams for all the vocal students. This I did for three consecutive years and was able to see a whole group of students progress through their course, and to watch them develop and blossom.

It was arranged that I should take on five post-graduate students, teaching on a Friday, so that I would travel up overnight from London on the Thursday night, breakfast in Glasgow at the excellent restaurant at Central Station, teach from 10 until 4, finishing in time to catch the last train back to London at around 5 pm. This journey would be five hours of comfort, with time to reflect, read, do paperwork, have dinner, arrive back at Euston, collect my car and be home by 11 pm. It did not always quite work out like that – more than once there were serious delays on the line and we suffered the usual frustrations and exhaustions. But by and large I enjoyed these weekly trips and they were surprisingly less fraught than some of the shorter journeys to closer destinations.

Not least of the pleasure of the job was the high quality of the students in Glasgow. I was lucky enough to teach some very talented young singers, one of whom is making her way up the ladder with Scottish Opera and singing principal roles (Rachel Hynes) and another, a superb Canadian soprano from Montreal (Karina Gauvin) who arrived with an already secure technique and developing artistry, who just needed a few pointers and some polish to her already considerable gifts. She has now made some prize-winning CDs, has a growing reputation as a recitalist, concert and opera singer and is set for a successful career. My teaching at the RSAMD came to an end in 1994 after five years.

I HAVE JUDGED PRIZES at all the London conservatoires over the years, and examined diploma candidates and final-year students at several of them. It is always a joy to hear some of the fine talent that continues to be nurtured at these establishments. One hopes there will be places for them all in the profession. I have faith that the cream rises to the top and that those with really exceptional gifts will find a niche for themselves in a crowded and competitive world – but the foot of the ladder is as congested as it ever was. There are probably more aspiring singers than there ever were but probably just as few with all that it takes to make a successful and lasting career as great artists.

Competitions

It has been a privilege over the years to be invited to serve on juries of international singing competitions. I have been back to Geneva for the Concours International. That was fascinating to see how it worked from the other side, as it were. It had a very good system of voting where, without going into detail, we were asked to vote for each candidate as 'oui', 'non' or 'éventuel'. This was carried through until first, second and third prize could be awarded. Often it has been that a first prize was easy to find but the runners-up were close and the result engendered much discussion and argument.

A new competition was set up in Athens in 1975 and I was invited to join the jury. The main award was the Maria Callas Prize and the competition was organised with much care and attention to detail by two Greek musicians, Louli Psichouli and Anna Koukouraki. They had the wisdom to divide the event into three categories, those of opera, oratorio and Lied. Singers could chose which category they wished to enter as their speciality, and they were expected to display ability to sing also in the two other categories. It was an admirable idea and gave opportunities to singers with preferences other than opera.

The proceedings were spread over a generous amount of time and we had the opportunity to enjoy the sights of Athens and to experience the generous Greek hospitality. I made a number of friends in the three years that I went there, and visited some of them later on at their holiday homes in Crete and Greece. Among fellow jury members was the lovely Italian soprano Graziella Sciutti – who later settled in London and taught at the Royal College of Music. She had been a firm favourite at Glyndebourne and sang there for many seasons. The celebrated tenor Giuseppe di Stefano was another jurist; he of course had been very closely associated with Maria Callas for many years. I have a vivid memory of lunching with him and his current ladyfriend and the Greek soprano Hero Palli at a waterside fish restaurant one beautiful day at Piraeus, when he talked very touchingly about his love for Callas and the hurt he felt when she virtually ignored him in New York after the start of her affair with Aristotle Onassis.

Another tenor who is remembered with pleasure and affection is Luigi

Alva, a superb artist and another Glyndebourne favourite. He and his charming wife were delightful companions. Hilde Zadek was another, and Arta Florescu from Romania became a good friend. Erich Kunz, the splendid Austrian baritone, was great fun, with Viennese charm and style.

Only two of the singers who competed stay in the memory, one a delightful Lieder singer from Lithuania who charmed with her beautifully poised voice and attractive personality – Sigite Trimakaite, and Nelly Miricioiou from Romania who impressed with her fine operatic performance, which she was later to reinforce here in London at Covent Garden.

BETWEEN 1962 AND 1982 a Mozart Memorial Prize was awarded by the Haydn-Mozart Society on nine occasions, of which I served on the jury three times, in 1975, 1978 and 1982. This prize was open to instrumentalists and singers, and it was wonderful to be able to hear many excellent woodwind players in the Mozart concertos, plus pianists and violinists, as well as the singers. Fellow jurors included Sir Peter Pears and Norma Burrowes for the singers, and regulars over the three years would be Harry Blech as Chairman, Emanuel Hurwitz, Angela Malsbury, Stephen Bishop-Kovasevic, Denis Matthews, Fanny Waterman, and others, of whom I particularly admired Nina Milkina, the beautiful pianist whose Mozart playing was such a joy. It was bliss to hear so much Mozart performed during the days of the competition – even if the performances were not always of prize-winning stature.

A SINGING COMPETITION which has been going for very many years takes place at ’s-Hertogenbosch in Holland. Roy Henderson was a frequent member of the jury and I was privileged to serve on it for three years in 1988, 1989 and 1990. This was another very well organised competition and great care was taken for the comfort and well-being of the competitors, and naturally of the jurors too. The little town was en fête during the week and for the first couple of days there was always a fun-fair in the square – just outside the hotel where I stayed! At this hotel one could splurge on a special item of confectionery – a sphere as a big as a cricket ball covered with chocolate and containing – as far as I could tell – pure whipped cream. It was called Bosschebolle and was a small piece of heaven.

My fellow jurors on the first occasion in 1988 were Menno Feenstra, who later moved to become casting director at Glyndebourne; the Norwegian soprano Ingrid Bjoner; Horst Günter from Germany, an old friend and

Jury at the International Vocalists' Competition, 's-Hertogenbosch, Holland, 1989: (left to right) Ingrid Bjoner, Helena Lazarska, Menno Feenstra, Horst Günter, myself, Robert Holl, Betty Allen, Jules Bastin

frequent visitor to London and the USA; the delightful Polish soprano Helena Lazarska, who teaches in Salzburg; Robert Holl, the fine Dutch Lieder singer; Jane Berbié, the French mezzo; and Lorenzo Alvary, bass from the USA.

Jurors in 1989 numbered again Feenstra, Lazarska, Bjoner, Günter and Holl, with newcomers Betty Allen, an African American singer who was director of a music school in Harlem, New York, and Jules Bastin from Belgium.

In 1990, we again had Betty Allen, Jules Bastin, and Helena Lazarska, with Menno Feenstra and newcomers Horeana Branisteanu from Switzerland, John van Kesteren from Holland and Hein van Royen, also from Holland.

There were over 100 competitors from 25 countries, with Russia being particularly well represented. In fact, the First Prize for Opera was awarded jointly to a Russian baritone and soprano, while no prize was awarded for

Oratorio, and three for Lied, first to a Japanese baritone, and second jointly to a Russian soprano and an American tenor.

I believe that for various reasons, mainly financial, the early 1990s saw the last years that the 's-Hertogenbosch International Competition for Singers was held as an annual event. Subsequently it has taken place irregularly and in a different format. This is a great pity as it had given opportunities to many young singers and it had a particularly comprehensive range, allowing for the three different specialisations. It is, however, interesting to note that the category of oratorio was never widely subscribed to, and the standard seldom reached that deserving of a first prize. English singers were reasonably well represented over the years and the list of winners includes a respectable number.

GLAA, AOTOS and others

It was in 1977 that I was invited to become a member of the Music Panel of the Greater London Arts Association (GLAA). I accepted with alacrity, thinking that it would be an opportunity to assist in allocating much-needed funds to worthwhile groups and individuals engaged in promoting classical music. For a while, so it seemed to be – the panel met about once a month and were constantly tiptoeing between the desire to encourage and support, and the constraints of the small budget. After a while though, things changed quite dramatically with the election of a new Labour controlled Greater London Council in 1981, with Tony Banks as Chairman of its Arts and Recreation Committee. Policy had been changing and we had already seen the first evidence of what was to become political correctness. Priority was given to 'community' arts and applications for funds were actively encouraged from ethnic groups of all kinds. This change in emphasis caught me unprepared. It would not have seemed quite so unfair had the struggling classical music clients not been sidelined; often scorn was poured on them as unenterprising, unimaginative, conservative and old-fashioned.

For months I and like-minded colleagues on the panel struggled against the tide. GLAA resisted an attempt at a takeover of its functions by the GLC, but a highly-charged special meeting agreed to adopt, among other policy statements put forward by the GLC, a resolution to fund community arts as its *main* priority. This was the last straw for me and I wrote a long, impassioned letter of resignation. The Music Panel at first refused to accept it, but my mind could not be changed and I regretfully severed all connection with GLAA.

It should perhaps be mentioned that the concept and practice of community arts and ethnic music has come a very long way since those days and attitudes among musicians have dramatically changed. Multicultural music thrives and develops, and today's scene would not have provoked the same reaction from myself and others, but would have engendered much admiration.

The most interesting part of my association with GLAA had been to serve every year from 1973 to 1981 on the audition panel for their Young Musicians programme which selected promising young artists for promotion in some recitals. This was fascinating and through it, and the ISM Young Artists' Scheme, we were able to hear the cream of the rising young musicians of the era. Looking back, I see that many of those whom we picked out have now become very well known and some have risen to the top of their particular tree, as instrumentalists and singers. For example among them was the clarinettist David Campbell, the Endellion Quartet, pianist Barry Douglas, saxophonist John Harle, cellist Steven Isserlis, soprano Alison Pearce, baritone David Wilson-Johnson, cellist Alexander Baillie and a host of others.

Also looking back on it now, after so many years, one can see how the social climate was changing and how arts funding was taking on a different complexion. The tribulations of the Arts Council and its relationship to various governments, the earlier establishment of the regional arts associations and their changing roles, the growth of business sponsorship of the arts, have all played major roles in carving up a very tiny cake into minuscule slices, if one views it in the wider picture of state funding. The bright spot on the horizon is now the addition of the national lottery into the picture, with already undreamed-of sums allocated to housing the arts and the promise of wider support being available in the long run. It is sad that our culture in the UK places classical music at such a low priority and that comparatively paltry sums are grudgingly doled out by successive governments. We are constantly comparing ourselves to other European countries in this respect and seem to come off worst in our state support for opera houses, and orchestras. Times are changing still and we continue to muddle and struggle along – but at what cost to our culture?

ANOTHER ORGANISATION with which I had a long-term connection was the National Music Council of Great Britain. I was invited to serve on it as an independent individual – that is, not representing another body – in 1966. The NMC was an umbrella organisation with a wide representation of British music organisations, amateur and professional, and was itself a member of the International Music Council whose headquarters were in Paris. Although the best of intentions informed its deliberations it was somewhat of a toothless tiger as there was no official funding and therefore no real power. It did achieve some useful things, one of which was a short film about British music made by the then chairman James Archibald, who was a film director. My services on this Council came to an end in 1976 when I resigned because of my new post at the ISM.

I should not here forget to mention that, shortly after my resignation from the ISM staff to take up the teaching appointment at the LCM, two new voluntary tasks came along which were to take up a great deal of time and energy.

FIRSTLY, IN 1986 I was elected Chairman of the Association of Teachers of Singing (AOTOS), after having served for many years on the committee. I was determined to put as much as I could into this and to take a leading role in the activities of the year. There are three events which take place

AOTOS Teacher Training Course, Harrow School, 1998: Mollie Petrie, Eileen Price and myself

regularly, which have been developed over the years – the Annual Conference which is held at different venues around the country and two one-day conferences in London in the spring and autumn. For years Norman Tattersall was Conference Director and did a wonderful job of organising venues and programmes.

Between us, we shared this task during my chairmanship, and mine was the major part in choosing the programmes and speakers. Administrative experience from the ISM was useful to inject a more business-like and professional briskness into the committee proceedings. The Annual Conference in 1987 was held at the Swan Hotel in Bedford. The Chairman's Address was entitled 'In at the deep end' (see Appendix B) and I also gave a session on the problems of Recitative and Ornamentation in performance and teaching. Among my guests were the distinguished Swedish specialist on breathing, Rolf Leanderson, who also gave a recital of Swedish songs; Ursula Vaughan Williams on 'Writing words for music'; the composer Roger Steptoe; the Canadian Michael Bawtree on Music Theatre; a masterclass by Thomas Hemsley and entertainments by the Alexandra Ensemble, by the celebrated girls' choir directed by Pamela Cook, and ending with Mollie Petrie's hilarious 'With a Frog in my Throat'. Guest of honour at the Annual Dinner was Sir Thomas Armstrong, who received a standing ovation for a speech extolling the merits of the great traditions of English singing. The Mayor of Bedford treated us to his humorous and enthusiastic thoughts on classical music, and gave us the memorable comment: 'Get-rich-quick pop music is the worst noise this side of the Pearly Gates'.

THE SECOND OF THE LARGE TASKS came in the same year when I was astonished to be approached by the ISM asking if I would accept the Presidency for the year 1988/9. I felt very greatly honoured and after a pause of about two seconds to consider the magnitude of the prospect, I accepted. It was, of course, a three-year undertaking as one became President Elect and Past President in the surrounding years. It was not the easiest of periods in the ISM's existence and it took all the tact and diplomacy one could muster to keep things on an even keel. Without going into details it is sufficient to say that there was dissent among some members and all was not well at Head Office either. My task was to chair meetings of the Executive Committee and the full Council, also to attend meetings of the three specialist sections. It is also traditional for the President to be invited to visit many centres around the country, and I tried to accept as many of these as possible. I went up to

Scotland to three Centres, over to Northern Ireland to the Belfast Centre, as well as many others in England and Wales. I lost count of the number of speeches but the evidence remains in a big ring-binder. As I became more used to public speaking, only a few notes and headings were needed, but at first I would laboriously write out a text and then try to memorise it. Speaking ad lib is now a great deal easier and more fun.

I wanted to hold my Annual Conference in London but realised that it could be a huge expense for out-of-town members to stay for three or four days. We decided to break with tradition and have a business-only conference with all the meetings, the AGM, the Annual Section Meetings held on one day. It was reasonably easy to organise and we booked the splendid Victorian hotel, the Hotel Russell, for the day. The Presidential Address was on the subject of 'Creation and Re-creation' (see Appendix A), and at the Annual Dinner in the evening the guest speaker was Jeremy Isaacs, then General Director of the Royal Opera House. As the hour approached we became a little anxious as Jeremy did not arrive for the reception. Just before the moment of going in to dinner, he turned up looking very worried and upset. It appeared that he had been delayed by a tragedy that had occurred earlier in the day at the Opera House. An accident on stage had resulted in the death of one of the stage-hands. Under the circumstances we were extremely grateful to Jeremy for turning up at all, and he went on to make an interesting speech, managing to hide his distress and to speak with calm and conviction.

At the end of the dinner I handed on the Presidential Badge to my successor, the composer William Mathias, not without some feelings of relief and lifting of a burden.

Conferences

It has been part of my progress as a teacher of singing to attend countless conferences – every year the annual get-togethers of the Association of Teachers of Singing, meetings of the British Voice Association and some of those of the National Association of Teachers of Singing of the USA, memorably at Philadelphia, at Tampa, Florida, and in Canada at Toronto.

It was in 1987 that a small group of NATS and AOTOS members got together with the idea of holding an international conference of voice teachers and as a result, the first International Congress of Voice Teachers took place in Strasbourg. The facilities there were excellent, as was to be expected in a city more than used to hosting international gatherings. A group of us from AOTOS travelled there together, creating something of a party spirit that set the tone for our off-duty times during the next four days. The impressive opening ceremony required that a representative of each country's organisation made a short speech of welcome. As the current chairman of AOTOS this task fell to me and I delivered a few 'well chosen' words in English and some of my best French. Undoubtedly the Conference is best remembered among AOTOS members, though, for an incident on our day of arrival. One of our distinguished lady members travelled from the airport with a group of Americans, NATS members. They checked in at their hotel but unaccountably our friend met a snag at the reception desk where they vowed she did not have a room reserved. After some altercation they gave her a room number and a key, upon which she found her room and entered. Her shock was profound when she was greeted by the sight of a very large, very dark gentleman lying naked in bed. Uttering a scream she dashed back to reception and a great fuss ensued. When it was all sorted out, it was discovered that she was in the wrong hotel after all. She has never ceased to be teased unmercifully to this day.

Encouraged by the success of this International Congress, the next one was arranged in Philadelphia in 1991. There we met all our old friends from NATS and the UK was represented by the then AOTOS Chairman Kenneth Bowen. Among the guest speakers was Ursula Vaughan Williams who gave a fine talk on poetry in song, and incidentally entertained royally in her hotel room, as did others who gave drinks parties in the evenings. The final recital was given by the English mezzo Sarah Walker with Malcolm Martineau, piano. The Strasbourg congress had ended with a recital by a comparatively unknown American baritone who has since become world famous – the handsome, charismatic young Thomas Hampson, who sang with such power and artistry that his lady audience was reduced to jelly. Tom was a student of our old friend Horst Günter.

Among the American singing teachers whom I got to know well over the years were the wise and kindly Bruce Lunkley from Texas, as large and generous a character as a true Texan is expected to be; James McKinney whose book *The Diagnosis and Correction of Vocal Faults* is an essential reference; Jack Coldiron, a tenor whose voice and artistry defied the passing of time; and Edward Baird, who with his friend, pianist Louise Lerch, have been frequent visitors to my home. All these came to the LCM to give workshops with our students and gave invaluable insights into vocal technique. Like most highly-placed teachers in the States they all had doctorates and professorships to various universities and music colleges. The interchange of knowledge between our two countries has played a great part in the improvement in the state of singing teaching, and has led to greater freedom in the exchange of information and experience between individual teachers, and also the spread of the results of scientific research into the workings of the vocal tract and all its ramifications.

After Philadelphia I joined with others on a weekend trip to Washington, where Derrick flew out to meet me and we spent a holiday in South Carolina with some Aston Martin-owning friends. He was an ophthalmic surgeon with an estate on which he grew a long-lost strain of rice called Carolina Gold, which he had discovered and brought back to cultivation. The guest-house was buried in the surrounding woods and each morning we would be awakened by a loud bang on the windows. To our horror we saw that a bird was flying repeatedly into the glass and we feared for its life, but apparently it was a well-known phenomenon, labelled by our hosts 'The Attack Cardinal', a gorgeously red-plumaged little bird with a short broad bill that it employed to give our wake-up call.

Prior to Philadelphia, I had flown from London to Seattle on 4 July, amid a huge firework display on arrival, to join Derrick and Justin who had been

The Edwards family and Christiana celebrate Derrick's 75th birthday, 1991

driving across from the east coast on a TransAmerica rally of vintage cars. We then drove up to Vancouver to stay with my cousins and to celebrate Derrick's 75th birthday, when we were joined by our daughter Michèle. It was a happy family occasion but sadly to be the last as within two months Derrick suffered a very severe stroke from which he never fully recovered, and the holiday in South Carolina was to be our last.

The third ICVT was held in Auckland, New Zealand, offering an opportunity of a visit down under where I had never been before. I flew out via San Francisco to spend a couple of days with friends and to do some sight-seeing, then direct to Auckland from Los Angeles.

The contingent from the UK was somewhat smaller this time, with the intrepid ones as ever in evidence. I was charged with task of presenting the AOTOS bid to hold the fourth Congress in London, a bid that was successful, so I was free to enjoy the rest of tour with a light heart. After the congress I visited friends in Wellington, a tenor and his wife who had lived in London and sailed their small boat back to New Zealand to settle back there. He was the chief presenter at their equivalent of Classic FM, presenting record programmes and interviews on a full-time basis.

The next leg of the trip took me to the South Island to Christchurch where I had been asked to do a week's teaching at the National Academy of Singing and Dramatic Art, a private training school founded and run by a singing teacher, Lois Clausen. There were some lively and interesting students on a new course that has since undergone a considerable change after joining a tertiary institution and gaining degree status.

I stayed with a most delightful family, supportive of the Academy, the wife, Mary, never losing an opportunity to take me sightseeing whenever there was time to spare. I could see why Derrick had at one time, before our marriage, considered going out to settle in New Zealand, which he had enjoyed while out there racing in their Grand Prix.

The next stop was Sydney where I stayed with friends, he the organist and master of music at Sydney Cathedral. I fell in love with the beautiful city where I felt immediately comfortable and at home. It was an added bonus that I discovered two former LCM students living there who had been contemporaries at college but were unaware of each others' presence. One was a lovely Australian soprano, the other a highly gifted Korean mezzo, who immediately planned joint recitals.

After a trip up to Queensland and the Great Barrier Reef, I flew up to Hong Kong for a weekend where the bass Michael Rippon, a colleague of many concerts and oratorios in England, was now living and who helped my sight-seeing. Next stop was Singapore for another week's teaching at a small music school run by an old friend. It was an illuminating experience to visit the many luxury hotels with their modern architecture and by contrast to visit the old Chinatown and the rebuilt Raffles Hotel. My hosts also took me for a day into Malaysia to a beautiful beach resort.

One is liable to meet people one knows unexpectedly in the Far Eastern crossroads of Singapore. One evening, while waiting for friends to park the car, I stood by a bank of elevators in one of the spectacular high-rise hotels. Suddenly a familiar face appeared. It was Philip Ledger, then Principal of the Royal Scottish Academy of Music and Drama, where I was currently a visiting teacher. He was on his way through to Japan on Academy business, and as surprised to see me as I was him. Other surprise encounters included colleagues travelling as examiners for the British examination boards.

It was with regret that I left Singapore on a flight back to London – it had been a wonderful trip and I felt I could have gone on for much longer exploring and experiencing new places ad infinitum. The perfect planning of the whole trip was due to my old friend Arthur Solomon, who took great pleasure in dovetailing flights and organising details of where I was to stay – to his credit, not a single hitch occurred.

HOWEVER, HARD WORK was awaiting me back home, since we now had three years in which to prepare for the fourth ICVT in London in 1997. I had been asked to take on the role of Programme Chairman, working with Norman Tattersall as Conference Director and Colin Schooling as Treasurer. This meant that I was responsible for planning the programme and booking speakers, performers and all participants – an enormous task. With the help of a few close colleagues we formed an Advisory Committee, and after one particular brain-storming session with Mollie Petrie, fine teacher and stalwart of AOTOS, we hit on the idea of themed days which developed into our final plan under the title *Voice through the Ages*.

Day 1: A Circle of Sound – this plotted the use of the voice from earliest history to the present day.

Day 2: Young Singers' Day.

Day 3: Singing Theatre Day – a collaboration between composer (Howard Goodall), librettist, director, speech coach to create a performance,

With Dame Joan Sutherland at the opening of the Fourth International Congress of Voice Teachers, London, 1997

co-ordinated by Mary Hammond from the Musical Theatre Course at the Royal Academy of Music.

Day 4: The Hearing Voice – exploring the relationship between ear and voice.

The final recital was to be given by the rising young mezzo Katerina Karneus who two years earlier had won the Cardiff Singer of the World Competition. Altogether the faculty for the Congress numbered forty-eight.

The next years built up to a climax when the Congress at last took place – we had settled on the Queen Elizabeth II Conference Centre at Westminster which we felt would be both central and popular with overseas delegates. I invited Dame Joan Sutherland to open the congress in the presence of the Dean of Westminster, and Dame Janet Baker closed the proceedings with an interview with Brian Kay. In between – I can hardly bring myself to say it even now just in case it brings bad luck – everything ran like clockwork. It seemed like a minor miracle and we all felt justifiably proud of all the hard work we had put into it. It was probably the last big challenge of my professional life – though there are still smaller hurdles being thrown at me in the quieter and more tranquil times.

Act IV, Scene 2
Last Projects and Finale

SO NOW WE ARE INTO THE FOURTH, and probably final stage of my working life – that of doing everything retired singers do – private teaching, adjudicating, examining – in fact whatever anybody thinks I might be useful for.

I have recently in the year 2000 been granted the Freedom of the City of London and in 2001 made a Liveryman of the Worshipful Company of Musicians.

My friend and colleague Tina Ruta, who is an Italian coach at Covent Garden and Paris Opera, and I have embarked on translating from Italian to English all the 19th-century Italian Composizione da Camera by Bellini, Donizetti, Verdi and Rossini.

The other great millennium project is to collect all the remaining recordings of my BBC broadcasts and have them transferred to CD, in which I am being helped by a former student, mezzo Claire Louise Lucas and her composer/pianist husband Jonathan Darnborough. From various sources, on reel-to-reel tape, cassettes, both home recorded or obtained officially from the BBC archives and the British Music Information Centre, these recordings are of variable quality and some have not survived, but Jonathan's skill as an editor and his and Claire's patience are making it a pleasurable task.

For several years I have been privileged to be a member of the Council of the Royal Philharmonic Society and have served on panels to select winners of the Society's Annual Awards in various categories of musicians – firstly the Solo Singers' Award and then as chairman of the Radio, TV and Video Award panel.

It has been a pleasure to support the newly founded Lennox Berkeley society. One of my few commercial recordings was of his *Four Poems of St Teresa of Avila*, and these beautiful songs have remained among my all-time favourites.

There are two music societies of which I am honoured to hold the Presidency. The first one was the Rochdale Music Society which puts on a first-class programme of six concerts a year – chamber music, recitals, occasionally orchestral; the second is the Aylesbury Festival Society which is a choral society performing an interesting and varied repertoire of choral works with young soloists. I sang with them in past years and now enjoy attending their concerts under their splendid young conductors Piers Maxim, and more recently, Justin Doyle.

There are some delightful students some of whom come up to London from distances as far as the Midlands and the South Coast to study. There are some with great talent, others who sing for the joy it gives them – and I continue to learn about the voice and how to help my singers achieve their potential. As many of us older singers say, 'If only I had known then (when I was singing) what I know now!' It is quite sad that when we have more insight and understanding both of the voice and of matters musical and artistic, our means of delivering them have deteriorated.

I have also recently started going over to the Isle of Man, at the invitation of very dear friends the Rev Arthur Solomon and his wife Ruth, to stay with

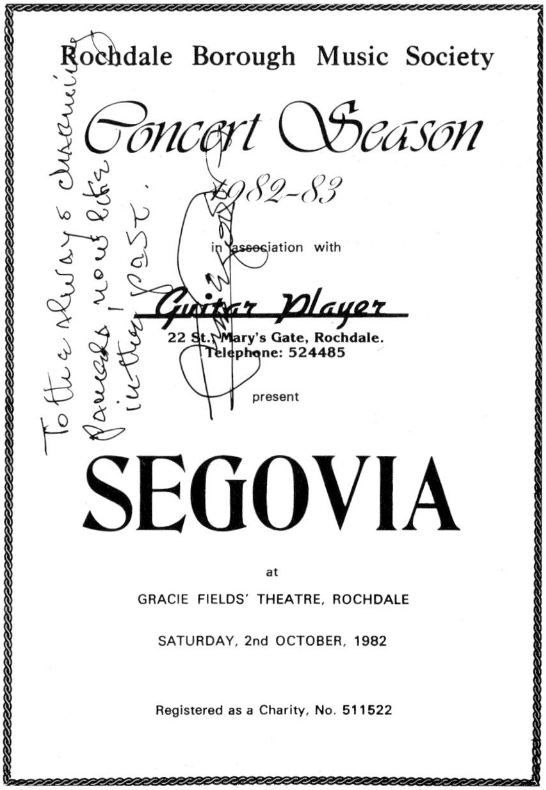
Rochdale Borough Music Society

Concert Season

1982-83

in association with

Guitar Player

22 St. Mary's Gate, Rochdale.
Telephone: 524485

present

SEGOVIA

at

GRACIE FIELDS' THEATRE, ROCHDALE

SATURDAY, 2nd OCTOBER, 1982

Registered as a Charity, No. 511522

I was able to renew an old acquaintance in 1982 – Segovia in Rochdale

With Prof in the garden of Ivor Newton House, Bromley, in 1998

At the Royal Philharmonic Society annual awards dinner, 1999 – Tony Fell, Chairman, myself and Clive Marks, sponsor

them and to take a series of workshops on French Song, initially, and general repertoire also, with some private teaching. There is a surprising richness of talent on the island and a great deal of love and enthusiasm for the art of singing, so it is always a great pleasure to work there, quite apart from the warm hospitality and attractive scenery.

The thought of a life without constant contact with singers and the delight of working with our enormous, rich, diverse repertoire of song and aria of every style, age and language, fills me with horror and I intend to carry on for as long as I am capable.

My home and garden give increasing pleasure and the old urge to travel is still there, though less so than in the past. If someone were to ring up tomorrow and ask me to go off to teach on the other side of the world, I daresay the answer would be 'when do you want me?'

London and Muscat 2000-2002

Appendix A
Creation and Re-creation

Presidential Address by Pamela Bowden
Incorporated Society of Musicians, March 1989

BEFORE STARTING ON MY PREPARED SCRIPT, I would like to say how interesting it has been during this day, while listening to the three excellent addresses given by the incoming Wardens of the specialist sections, to note how often their thoughts have chimed in with what I am about to say. To take one example, the new Warden of the MES took as his theme 'Integration' and the importance of musicians working together in all spheres, which is a matter dear to my own heart. Similarly, the other two Wardens seemed to tune in to further mutual wavelengths. So often it appears that there are thoughts and themes in the air, like music, for our antennae to pick up at the same time.

As musicians we are all involved in one or both of the subjects I have chosen for my address. It is a truism, and also a simplification, to say that composers are the only real creators; the rest of us owing our existence to them. There were gasps followed by applause when composer Nigel Osborne told the audience of orchestral managers, promoters, agents and assorted others at this year's Association of British Orchestras Conference, 'To hell with you. I don't need you. You need me.' But was he right? Only partly, I think.

The task of the performer is to recreate the composer's intentions. The skilled and talented will at the same time add some indefinable quality of their own to enhance and clarify the composer's indications – for indications, however detailed, are really all that the limitations of our only system of putting musical sounds on paper allow. The re-creation process involves a good performer very deeply with imagination and intuition coupled with an acquired understanding of style, performance practices of other eras, and often with research, particularly into early music where realisation and ornamentation can lead them to original creativity of their own. The creativity that one experiences as a performer is justified in that one may be creating, for an instant in time, an atmosphere, a memory, a mood and a response in the listener.

Britten once said,

'A musical experience needs three human beings: a composer, a performer and a listener, and unless these three take part together there will be no musical experience . . . The experience will be more intense and rewarding if the circumstances correspond to what the composer intended. The further one departs from these circumstances, the less true and more diluted is the experience likely to be.'

Singers are unique in that they owe an equal debt to a second creative force – the poet. It is arguable that poetry, when brought to life from the written page, is given added tension and poignancy by being set to music, and the marriage of two art forms created by two great artists results in a force greater than the sum of the two elements. I am certain this is true when a masterly composer sets fine poetry – when Wolf or Schubert set Goethe or Heine, when Britten sets Michelangelo or Blake – and it is true that when such a composer sets less than the finest verse it is elevated by the genius of his imagination, as we observe in some of the songs of Mozart. Grieg said,

'When I compose a song, my first concern is not to make music but, first and foremost, to do justice to the poet's intentions. I have tried to let the poem reveal itself and indeed to raise it to a higher power.'

Against that, Satie wickedly wrote,

'The musician is perhaps the most modest of animals but he is also the proudest. It is he who has invented the sublime art of ruining poetry.'

Because of our service to two Muses, can we say that singers are doubly re-creative? I like to think so. A song recital by Fischer-Dieskau or Elly Ameling has the potential to involve us in a spiritual experience on two levels that can combine to scale heights of human expression, heights less likely to be achieved by purely musical or literary means, though I know that is a controversial statement. Perhaps I should say here that I have in mind the Bach *Passions*, Elgar's *Gerontius* and other great choral works as well as the song repertoire.

Singers have to rationalise the process which W H Auden describes in his words: 'A verbal art like poetry is reflective; it stops to think. Music is immediate, it goes on to become.' So our reflections and thoughts have to be given immediate voice and translated into the fleeting musical moment that 'becomes' for a brief period and is gone again.

Teachers may be said to be creative – not in the sense of bringing into being a work of art of the imagination (though, let us face it, some students defy all one's imagination!) but in the sense that they create the conditions in which the singer or instrumentalist may thrive and grow in skill and in musical understanding. Students need stimulation of their imagination and curiosity to explore the standard repertoire and then to proceed more adventurously; to be encouraged to find out what is happening in contemporary composition and to seek out a wide variety of styles and techniques. Young people need teachers who are able to stimulate, who are themselves interested in the new or the unfamiliar, who can still be excited by new music, by the newly discovered, even the exotic. If the teacher becomes stuck in a time warp and loses that sense of adventure and creativity, the student may inherit these limitations and be confined for the rest of his musical life in a blinkered world of prejudice.

Our conservatoires should regard as a vital part of their job the cross-fertilisation of ideas and the stimulation of creativity, not only in composition but also in performance techniques. There is unrivalled opportunity for all the disciplines to work together among singers and instrumentalists and, where they exist, with departments of drama, art and design, dance and ballet.

Sometimes these forces are brought together but all too often the various disciplines work on their own in isolation and attempts at cooperation meet with only partial success. Of course there are reasons for this, financial or logistical, but inertia can also prevail. You don't have to be a bus ride apart to be isolated from each other. Some people manage it in the same building. We all know what happens in the commercial world, in the theatre and particularly in opera, where art, drama and music all work together. Are we doing the job as fully as we might for our students when they leave us without some understanding and experience between the disciplines? We already do this to some degree but it is my belief that it should be a much richer experience.

Re-creation may also be read as recreation, so that in the performance of music, to the performer as to the listener, enjoyment and refreshment are essential elements, something which we sometimes tend to forget in the intensity of preparation, anxiety and tension experienced by the performer. Milton saw music as a valuable recreation for students between academic work and physical activity. He wrote in his *Tractate of Education*, in one of the longest sentences ever,

'The interim of unsweating themselves regularly, and convenient rest before meat may both with profit and delight be taken up in recreating and composing their travailed spirits with the solemn and divine harmonies of music heard, or learned, either while the skilled Organist plies his grave and fancied descant in lofty fugues, or the whole Symphony with artful and unimaginable touches adorn and grace the well-studied chords of some choice composer . . .'

The sentence continues to embroider his theme for another forty-seven words!

Of course, the creation and re-creation of an art form calls for technical expertise as a first requirement. There is great store set, quite rightly, on the acquisition of technique and this is manifestly justified, for without mastery of the instrument or voice the artist is unable to realise to the full that which his innate musicality and intelligence tell him to convey. To interpret with freedom and to be spontaneous, to throw new light on a passage on the spur of the moment, need confidence that the fingers, the breath, the larynx will respond freely and answer to the brain's command. This is self-evident to every musician – and yet one wonders if we have already gone too far, have we paid too high a price for the startling increase in technical standards over the past 30 years or so? There has always been breathless amazement at feats of virtuosity, Liszt, the young Mozart, Jenny Lind, Paganini, all astonished in their time – and each one had varying degrees of magic with which to enchant their audiences. Today as ever there is no mistaking the real communicator, the interpreter with something special to say – but the rungs of the professional ladder are cluttered with many competent soloists who seem to get by on technical prowess and little else.

Some time ago I attended the finals of a prestigious singing competition at which we were treated to short recitals by half-a-dozen highly competent singers. Their voices were well-trained, they had chosen their songs with care and some out-of-the-way items were offered to add interest to their programmes. On the whole their platform presentation was adequate. At the end, a lady sitting next to me who went regularly to this competition and was a keen lover of singing, turned to me and said sadly, 'That was all very well but where has the beauty gone?' I think that is a question we all ask from time to time and is to me an indication that while our standards of technical training, particularly for instrumentalists, may well have reached great heights, our artistic standards can never be taken for granted.

ISM – the familiar acronym for our Society – has been given other interpretations from time to time. We have made up different slogans to fit it, some funny, some highly irreverent, as it should be among such an irreverent group of people as musicians. One recently suggested to me was 'Isn't Singing Marvellous?' Perhaps we should hold a competition for the best? Another of more general application could be 'Is our Standard Maintained' – a trifle clumsy but it poses an important question for our Society when we remember our ISM aim 'to uphold the honour and interests of the musical profession' and that we exist for the promotion of the art of music – in which the question of standards is implicit, and which identifies the nature of professionalism as not only earning a living but also in developing high standards.

On a broad front we are concerned with all kinds of standards; those of teaching, performing, composing, administering, behaviour towards our students, colleagues and the public. The fact that we are members of the Society confirms our commitment to these ideals and we understand just how much effort has to go into the maintenance and promotion of excellence, in every form of human activity, not alone in music.

We have recently been living in the age of the easy option. They say that it has been in the interests of encouraging creativity and stimulating the imagination that old-fashioned methods of learning by rote have been dismissed as unimaginative, dull, stultifying. Numeracy has no longer been based on learning tables, grammar has not been taught nor verbs declined, sonnets not required to be memorised. What a disservice has been done to our young people in the process and how sad has been the decline in general educational standards, when today many school-leavers are said by industrialists to be unemployable. Without an official arbiter for the English Language such as the French have in their Académie Française, there is grave danger of our wonderfully rich and expressive language being diminished in common usage to a fraction of its vocabulary and misuse and mis-spelling becoming widespread. It is commonplace to see young assistants in shops having to use a calculator to multiply two by ten or make a simple addition. At long last this nettle has been grasped and the new requirements of the core curriculum should remedy our basic educational standards for the future. This will take time and sadly at least one generation has been deprived and disadvantaged in the meantime.

What one can perceive as the most disturbing element has been the failure to give due importance to the value of mental discipline, which is where early training in music scores and where one of the greatest blessings of music education lies. It is well known that music graduates are among the most sought-after group when it comes to employment and they are hardly ever at a loss to find work outside music should they wish to do so. This must be a matter of some consolation to those of us concerned with training young musicians in the conservatoires when we know perfectly well that only a fraction of our students will be able to find a niche within the music profession, particularly as performers. It is sad that there will soon be a considerable shortage of music specialists in schools so it follows that in our music colleges we should be turning our attention to providing well-trained general and specialist teachers. I believe we have a long way to go and not enough importance is attached to excellence in training teachers nor sufficient emphasis placed on guiding them away from the bright mirage of the pot of gold at the rainbow's end of a performing career into the very real satisfaction of the pedagogue – albeit with a flake of gold as a reward instead of the pot. I use the word 'pedagogue' in its classical sense and not with awful Dickensian connotations.

With all its excellent work for private teachers and teachers in education, the ISM is successfully raising their image and self-esteem, and promoting increasingly high standards by its activities. New moves arising out of last year's Annual Conference are working in the direction of encouraging the maintenance and improvement of performance skills among teachers, which must lead to higher teaching standards in their turn. The Society's Codes of Ethics, of which three have been devised and brought into practice during this year, can only serve to underline the constant pursuit of excellence.

As for the future, the ISM is finding itself in a highly defensive position in having to adapt to a rapidly changing society. Although Britain's entry into the EEC did not bring about such drastic loss of employment and increase in competition from abroad among musicians as was feared at that time, we still do not know precisely what will be the effect of the open market in 1992. They say that the best form of defence is attack so we must be ready to take an active lead. We must, in this shrinking world, go out and make contact with colleagues in other countries, not just individually as many of our international artists already do, but as a group reaching out to similar groups with the same profession and the same deep concern for our art. We already have members who are also members of international specialist organisations such as ESTA, EPTA, and EVTA, the new European Voice Teachers Association. These are vital allies of the ISM and must be regarded as complementary in their work for their own disciplines to the overall umbrella of the ISM. I have always thought the ISM was unique in its coverage of all branches of the music profession, and so it was until recently. Now, in the USSR, we hear that glasnost has permitted Russian musicians to form a similar association that we would like to contact to, we hope, our mutual benefit.

On the matter of international standard pitch we must continue to speak of our concern about the arbitrary rise now being established by orchestras world-wide. While early music groups are returning to baroque instruments at baroque pitch, symphony orchestras are departing from the standard A=440 in a quite deliberate policy, each orchestra at its own preferred pitch, of responding to modern liking for brighter and more brilliant tone. I have already voiced the dismay of singers elsewhere and it was encouraging to note that a public protest was made last year by a group of celebrated singers at La Scala, Milan. We are plunged right back to the situation at the end of the last century when even more violent fluctuations of pitch were commonplace. The famous laryngologist, Cathcart, who helped Sir Henry Wood finance the first Promenade Concerts at the Queen's Hall in 1894, would only do so providing that 'the orchestral instruments should be tuned to French pitch and not to the higher concert pitch' as was then usual. The consequences of this upward drift can be catastrophic for singers and can make life difficult for others, particularly in tuning to organs and elderly pianos.

One is reminded, not entirely relevantly, of the story told by Jack Brymer in his book *From Where I Sit.* The conductor George Szell, in a speech, is quoted as saying,

'Ladies and Gentlemen, I want you to know that during my stay in London your orchestras have been most generous to me. When tuning, all I asked for was one pitch. You have invariably given me two or three at least.'

For many years those with some vision have been prophesying a more leisured and cultivated society in the future, a society with time for recreation. Now the likelihood of that vision coming true creeps a little nearer and property developers are making provision for all kinds of leisure, sports and cultural activities in their major schemes. One of the latest to be publicised is a proposal for a London development with provision for a new, medium-sized opera theatre. The inspirer of this scheme is quoted as saying, 'Cultural business will be the business of the 21st century – what else will we have to do?'

Since the 'cultural business' is also our business, we must see to it that we have a stake in that leisured society for our own and our children and our grandchildren's sake, remembering, and constantly reiterating, that it is music and the arts which make an incalculable contribution to the national income, are one of the best investments in terms of value for money on a national scale, and are among our most successful exports. It is our ISM members who will be looking forward and preparing the ground for future development and success. 'Your young men shall see visions and your old men shall dream dreams' – words which Elgar so movingly set in *The Kingdom.*

I have wandered over a wide area in enlarging on the theme of creation and re-creation, with emphasis upon performing and teaching rather than composition as befits my own experience. But, according to Stravinsky, 'Too many pieces finish too long after the end.' His advice is good and I must finish with the end of this piece.

Appendix B
In at the Deep End

Chairman's Address by Pamela Bowden
AOTOS Annual Conference, 1987 (edited version)

ARISTOTLE SAID: 'Music is taught worldwide in a very hazardous and dangerous manner.'

When I was thinking about a subject for this talk, I first thought I might use that as a title, but then it occurred to me that as musicians our whole lives seem to be spent diving in at the deep end. Imagine a diver preparing for a difficult dive – he stands on a board, mentally and physically alert – getting ready in mind and body for the test ahead. The athlete is well trained, he has rehearsed the movements time and time again, the muscles are well balanced and in control, the mind is concentrating on only one thing, the next vital moments of the deep breath, the leap, the twist and turn and then the clean plunge down into the water and finally surfacing – to swim to the side, clamber out and start all over again, climbing up to the diving board.

We can easily see the parallel here with our experience as singers. Mind and body trained – years of practise and preparation – then the leap off into the performance. In a sense then, every time we walk on to a platform, that is a dive into the deep end. We know what we have to do, we are as well prepared as possible, we have been working for this moment for years right up to the minute we step out in front of the public. We stand in the wings, take a deep breath – and the moment arrives.

And yet, despite all the training and preparation, there is always an element of uncertainty. The diver knows he is not going to hit his head on the bottom of the pool – but there is always an outside chance that he might. He has not up to now misjudged a twist or turn and landed smack on the water, winding or injuring himself – but he might. So we singers are never entirely certain – so many things might go wrong, from forgetting the words to missing the conductor's beat, or to some unexpected disaster on a top note – or just not being in good form. Perhaps not the danger to life and limb risked by the diver – but real enough danger to self-esteem, confidence and reputation. Sometimes we may even feel like the idiots who jump off the Clifton Suspension Bridge or the Eiffel Tower on a piece of elastic!

I sometimes think that we musicians, in addition to our inadequate fees, should be paid 'danger money'.

I had a wonderful life as a singer – even if I spent most of it with my head just under water – and I arrived gasping at the shallow end a few years ago.

In preparation for this time I started doing a little private teaching some years before I ended my singing career. I had not earlier been interested while making my way and then being busy, and it was more out of a feeling of duty – and advice from my friends – that I started with the odd pupil or two. Those first pupils got from me a carbon copy of my own teacher Roy Henderson. I believed – and still do – that his teaching was basically sound. He had a marvellous ear (the most valuable of a teacher's gifts), the highest standards gained from his own successful career, and a commonsense approach which appealed to me. He had a fine sense of style and was able to teach one to work in great detail on say, a Schubert song, carefully shaping each phrase, with subtle gradations of dynamics, and the most meticulous attention to the colouring of word, phrase and putting it all together to create the atmosphere of each song. He was insistent above all on clarity of diction and also that everything must be memorised. He always said that you did not really know a piece well enough unless you had it from memory, and never allowed his students to use a score. Even if you took one on to the platform to comply with tradition or in an ensemble, the work must be memorised.

He was ahead of his time in that he was always interested in using scientific research to back up his work and was one of the first to use an oscilloscope to demonstrate the vibrato, or lack of, or wobble in a voice to any student who needed convincing. He would get students to sing into the microphone and see for themselves on the screen how the pattern varied according to the width of vibrato, intensity of sound and smoothness of legato. This was really only to prove a point and was not used on any regular basis as a teaching aid. We are, of course, very familiar nowadays with these graphic examples, and of a much more sophisticated nature, but he was a pioneer in his interest in scientific and medical information being used for the benefit of the singer. Later he was one of the first to use a video camera in his studio and we all know how helpful this is – again to prove matters of posture, expression, gesture – saving a lot of time in convincing students that they really do lean forward the moment they start to sing, or that they really do need to relax the jaw, or whatever. Again, fairly basic stuff but quite new twenty-five years ago. He had successes at many levels – notable examples were of course

Kathleen Ferrier, Jennifer Vyvyan and Norma Procter – and there was so much to get from him for those who could.

My learning process as a teacher, then, started from this base, and as my teacher developed and changed in his methods and ideas over the twenty years I studied with him, so my own have gone on to develop and, I hope, advance. It would be interesting to know how differently each one of us works now from, say, ten years ago. Given a particular vocal problem, how would you tackle it today as opposed to earlier? Would you do the same – are you convinced you have the answer that works and needs no modification? Have you experimented a lot, trying out new ideas, or are you happy that you do not need to seek any other ways of doing things?

Sometimes, I have thought, 'Ah, that's it! Now I have got it – I know this is what it is all about. That's the answer!' Well, that happy certainty usually lasts all too short a time, or until the next revelation. Hopefully these inspirations do not contradict each other but go on adding to our store of information – dare I say 'tricks of the trade' – ways of coaxing the best out of a wide variety of minds and bodies.

I now find that I teach quite differently from my teacher, using different ways of trying to get to the same point – because the goal is still the same, and above all firstly he, and then experience, taught me – and all of you – just what we are aiming to bring out in our pupils. First, the technical ability to allow their voices to resonate freely, securely and evenly throughout the optimum range; second, the musical skills to enable them to sing in all styles ranging through Bach, Brahms and Bartók, or Monteverdi, Mozart and Messiaen; thirdly the love of words and response to poetry without which no singer is complete. But first and foremost, the singer has to have a good sound technique at his service – to fall back on in times of trouble – but mainly because without it his interpretative and artistic ideas cannot be carried out and he is constantly frustrated and impotent, unable to communicate.

We heard a superb example of the singer's art in the recital at Strasbourg by Thomas Hampson, the young American baritone. He held six hundred people – singing teachers too – in the palm of his hand. In a wide-ranging programme of Scarlatti, Wolf, Debussy, Barber and Strauss he displayed not only a fine, well-balanced, really outstanding voice, but a knowledge of style, a sensitivity, subtlety in handling of the words – every one clean as crystal and impeccable languages – and also marvellous presence; every look, gesture, tilt of the head, angle of the body had meaning. When he sang *Anakreons Grab*, one could hardly breathe, so magical was the atmosphere.

Here was great artistry that brought tears to the eyes of many of us and must surely be a true inspiration for our efforts.

Then we come home and start again with a new batch of first years – down to earth with a bump but something still resonating at the back of the mind, never to be lost.

The recent subject for discussion in our magazine 'Singing' is concerned with the hypothesis: 'The interpretative aspect of singing should not be attempted before the technical side is completely mastered'.

I think that to restrict the remit of the singing teacher to that of the voice trainer – which in some schools of thought seems to be the case – is a waste of resources and a denigration of that teacher as an artist.

To suggest that a singer should go through any period of training, let alone the time needed to perfect a technique, without reference to the musicianship and interpretative understanding needed for good performance is to me a nonsense. I certainly do not believe that the great school of bel canto was founded on months and years of working with vocalise, without reference to the music they were eventually to perform. That is indeed relegating the voice to a clockwork nightingale – and I am perfectly aware of Porpora's page of vocal exercises on which he is supposed to have kept Caffarelli for five years. I find that all my teaching is related to things musical and interpretative right from the start. Sometimes we have to concentrate hard on certain aspects of technique, trying to eliminate a fault or working towards the next 'plateau' and sometimes that leads to such dull and spiritless renditions of songs that one is brought up very sharply and one has to remind the student not to forget the general in search for the particular. Then by re-finding the composer's intentions, we often find that the technical work also falls into place and the imagination once again helps it all to work properly.

I went to the finals of the Kathleen Ferrier Memorial Scholarship in the Wigmore Hall earlier this year and heard some very accomplished young singers. There were seven competitors, aged between twenty-one and twenty-five, all of whom sang demanding programmes with reasonable techniques, evidence of careful musical preparation and presentation. We heard voices trained to carry above all, singers anxious to have a big sound fully capable of being heard above the orchestra in the opera house – voices often stretched to the utmost – the great fear of being accused of having a voice too small to be useful. I am afraid that we are in danger of throwing out the baby with the bathwater. That excessive concern with size, with weight, leads us more and more to forget that elusive beauty of tone, that freshness in the voice that can so easily be lost and sacrificed to volume. I know that all of us can recall examples of this imbalancing of the vocal means – voices of great early beauty and promise that have deteriorated all too soon. But it is worrying when we find students striving to out-sing each other, not in musicianship, beauty of tone, depth of understanding, but just in decibels.

Actors know all about the use of dynamics in creating atmosphere – they are much freer than we are to vary them at will, and to vary their timing too, not being bound by the stave and the barline. So very often the most attention-catching moments are those of quiet intensity. A clever singer also uses a wide range of dynamics and in so doing the extremes of the range appear to be greater than they are – the loud seems louder when contrasted with a very soft pianissimo.

Once the vocal technique is adequate, it becomes possible to produce greater volume and intensity up to the limit of one's resources, and all too often these days that is the be-all and end-all of what is expected of the singer. Loudest is best. Not bel canto but 'can belto'. But not only is this necessity for big sound making the singer's life increasingly difficult and increasingly short, it is posing problems for the singing teacher in protecting the voices, minimising harm and helping the gifted professional singer to prolong a career beyond his thirties.

We all know that the development of the symphony orchestra, and more recently of electronics has been partly responsible for this – and we have been bemoaning it for years – but what can we do about it? Probably not much, but if we don't raise our voices to protest, who will? Not the young singers with careers at stake and who dare not refuse work – unless we can somehow convince them of the danger to their voices. It is time to stop making impossible demands on singers, so often for reasons that are purely commercial, but I fear that managements will not listen when their pockets are affected.

It is wonderful to hear a great voice riding easily over an orchestra on the operatic stage; even more difficult, on the concert platform. It is a thrilling and uplifting experience. But these great voices are rare – and there are so many performances to cast in opera houses world-wide. There are many fine singers with smaller physiques who find it very hard to sustain such big singing – who mánage it for just so long and then realise they have used up, all too quickly, their capital resources.

There are fine artists whose work is on a smaller scale who nowadays find it possible to survive only in the fields of early or contemporary music – sadly it is no longer possible to make an international career as a Lieder singer or in oratorio.

Now, I am not suggesting that we should not continue to develop voices for good size and range, to make them viable for performances in big theatres and halls. Of course we must – anything less would be impractical and we have to aim for the very best. But I am saying that agents and managements, conductors and music directors must be constantly reminded that no voice should be pushed beyond its natural limits – that unlike electronics, no amount of research will bring bigger and bigger sounds from the human frame.

It is the message of the words that distinguishes the singer from the instrumentalist, and the all-important factor is that those words must be clearly audible and capable of colour and inflection. This cannot be achieved at high volume – or high pitch.

How can we persuade the conductor that by adjusting with more sensitivity to the words he would be able to create the right conditions for a performance of far greater emotional and intellectual intensity – allowing the singer to release the vocal mechanism from a sometimes intolerable tension, while still allowing a highly-strung but more flexible flow of tone?

Even Wagner insisted on a cover for the orchestra pit at Bayreuth – perhaps that would be a cheap(ish) and easy answer to some of these problems too. For at Bayreuth, as the following extract from an article in *Classical Music* (15 August 1987, ed. Graeme Kay) describes,

'[The music] . . . is compressed by a sound-board rather like the hinge-plate of a letter-box, then travels up round the conductor's head to be projected back towards the singers by a cowl which also masks the musicians from the audience's view. By the time the sound has blended with the voices and travelled out towards the spectators, it is perfectly in balance.'

We all know of some honourable exceptions – the 'singers' conductors' – who can be relied on to be on your side. And in early music, matters are eased by the use of lighter orchestration and baroque instruments tuned to lower pitch. But alas, this is too often an excuse for bad singing of another kind – colourless, unsupported and dull – albeit light and flexible. Again, there are honourable exceptions of course, and recently I have heard some very good performances by early music ensembles – our players in particular are among the best in the world.

It is time to put a stop to the insidious creeping-up in pitch, frequency by frequency, that has been taking place in symphony orchestras world-wide.

Norman Punt, in *The Singer's and Actor's Throat,* says,

'Only sing roles within your tessitura – the highest pitch demanded of operatic tenors and sopranos cannot be achieved, except in rare instances, without causing the vocal mechanism to act in a forcible manner which is liable to injure the larynx. So strongly did Cathcart – himself a singer's laryngologist of repute – feel about this, that when he helped to finance the first Promenade Concert at the Queen's Hall in 1894, he insisted that "the orchestral instruments should be tuned to French pitch and not to the higher concert pitch", as was then usual!

'Many sopranos can only reach the desired high notes with sufficient volume by employing the glottal shock attack – hence their being the group most liable to nodules.'

The European and American orchestras are the worst culprits, having lifted their pitch from the agreed standard of A=440 to, in some cases, A448. One can easily understand the added stress on the soprano and tenor voices in particular, on the coloratura mezzo and the high Verdi baritone as well.

What can we do? There is currently a move to try and persuade orchestras to return to the still-established standard pitch of A440. This is a problem because ears become attuned to brighter resonances, instrument manufacturers now tune their woodwind to higher pitch – incidentally causing problems in schools where pianos are often old and cannot be tuned up to the higher pitched new flutes and recorders.

I feel that we should support this movement to lobby for a return to A440 – there is already talk of it – and enquiries were made a year or two ago by the ISM, which contacted all the main symphony orchestras.

Secondly – we should be brave enough to speak out whenever we hear of singers being unacceptably pushed into unsuitable roles, too many performances and so on. We as an association should be able to protest to managements and agents – anyone who will listen – and of course use our individual voices, too.

I was slightly cheered by attending the finals of the Walter Grüner Lieder Competition. Here, the young singers were trying above all to create atmosphere and using their voices – despite some technical deficiencies – with subtlety – able to use floating head tones and phrasing with imagination. Not always successfully but at least working towards it. This is the best type of competition – demanding in repertoire with a huge number of songs to learn – but also demanding on the use of the voice in detail and working with the German language – ideal for the young singer.

If we are lucky enough to have pupils who are really likely to succeed, we must make sure they are psychologically ready for success as well as musically ready. Not many of us are lucky enough to have students of such high calibre. But how fortunate we are when the students arrive at music college really well prepared and given an excellent foundation by our colleagues who start them off in their early days. This is vitally important – such is the value of AOTOS that we can meet each other and learn together. The scientific background to what we teach is becoming so much more available to us all and this must lead to increased awareness of how best to develop fine voices on a sound foundation – instinct backed up by medical and acoustical knowledge. We hear many scientific papers that are extremely interesting and valuable as pure information, but what we now need is practical application of that information – how we can best put all this new research into practice. This is surely another way forward for AOTOS, in close collaboration with other bodies such as the Voice Research Society and of course the other international societies like NATS and newly-formed European ones. We have to jump in at the deep end too.

I think it would be fitting to end with a quotation from some words by Yehudi Menuhin in his preface to the Music Guide on *Voice*, in which he says:

'May the human voice continue to stir us . . . it is our defence against mechanical repetition, against the mindless inhuman noise barrage, against electronic imitation and the ruthless, insensitive staccato of the machine gun. In the song may be heard suffering and joy transmuted, a living record of our humanity.'

It is obvious that, over the centuries from Ancient Greece to now, music is still being taught – and performed – in a hazardous and dangerous manner!

Some Press Opinions

Oratorios

St Matthew Passion *(Bach)*
'Outstanding among the soloists was Pamela Bowden who sang her arias warmly and affectingly.'
Daily Telegraph, London
'The most satisfying parts of the performance were those in which Miss Pamela Bowden was singing the alto arias.'
The Times, London

St John Passion *(Bach)*
'The English contralto Pamela Bowden, who brought to this performance a rich variety of expression and tonal beauty, gave to the aria "Es ist vollbracht" a sublime spirituality with her magnificent artistry.'
Berlingske Tidende, Copenhagen
'A beautiful, bright contralto, sang her aria really movingly.'
Zurich

B Minor Mass *(Bach)*
'The sustained beauty of her Agnus Dei was a thing to remember.'
Country Life, London

Messiah *(Handel)*
'. . . the magnificent contralto, Pamela Bowden . . . brilliant performance.'
Nieuws van de Dag, Amsterdam

Vespers *(Monteverdi)*
'Nigra Sum, superlatively delivered by Pamela Bowden, created one of the most moving and splendid additions to the whole Festival.'
Yorkshire Post

Solomon *(Handel)*
'The rich, big voice of Pamela Bowden's alto showed us the English oratorio tradition in the most beautiful manner and with noble majesty in the part of Solomon, with artistic, musical and dramatic feeling in the vocal line.'
Aktuelt, Copenhagen

Concerts

'Pamela Bowden, a soloist of special quality ... a splendid control of tone and a clarity of diction which brought out the finest subtleties of meaning.'

De Tijd-Maasbode, Amsterdam

Alto Rhapsody *(Brahms)*

'the most distinguished performance in the *Alto Rhapsody*, her fine contralto voice negotiated the wide intervals with exemplary skill.'

Daily Telegraph, London

'... an exceptionally pure and even contralto ... used it with intensity as well as dignity ...'

The Times, London

'Pamela Bowden's movingly beautiful account of the solo part a memorable performance.'

Sunday Times, London

Bath Festival Concert with Boulanger and Menuhin

'Pamela Bowden's account of the solo part was sensitive and articulate.'

The Times, London

Romeo et Juliette *(Berlioz)*

'Appealingly sung ... she succeeded in producing the pure, uncompromising vowel sounds the French words demand.'

Country Life, London

Festival du Marais, Paris: Les Nuits d'Été *(Berlioz)*

'Profoundly sung.'

France Soir

Altenberglieder *(Berg)*

'She dealt with this exacting music as though to her it was set in the clearest imaginable perspective . . . An altogether splendid performance.'

The Times, London

Diary of one who disappeared *(Janácek) (Sung in Czech)*

'The mezzo-soprano voice held lustre and beauty of feeling.'

Yorkshire Post

Recitals

'. . . programme showed lively intelligence of the artist in differing climates evoked by composers such as Arne, Purcell, Berkeley and Samuel Barber. In particular must be mentioned her very moving account of Schumann's

Frauenliebe und Leben in which the artist portrayed, in excellent German diction, all its touching, tender emotions, all its deepest lyricism.'

Journal de Genève

'Her singing is remarkable for its legato and beauty of phrasing. Her interpretation of songs by Schubert showed an unusual and subtle comprehension of Lieder singing and by means of her splendid technique Miss Bowden's artistry revealed new beauties.'

Daily Telegraph, London

'It seems that a singer of modern music has been discovered, for she met the cool, detached climate of this music with a skilful declamation and moderated use of her voice.'

Düsseldorfer Nachrichten

'Pamela Bowden, a young English contralto, had a great success at her debut in some complicated vocal works by Luciano Berio and Stravinsky. The audience witnessed her phenomenal musicality and sure sense of style.'

Der Mittag, Düsseldorf

'A lovely contralto voice of extraordinary charm, natural and profound ... Pamela Bowden holds her audience in an atmosphere of refinement and freshness, imbued with emotion.'

Journal de Genève

Opera

Glyndebourne Festival Opera: Yevgeny Onegin *(Tchaikovsky)*
(Sung in Russian)

'Pamela Bowden gave a very beautifully judged performance.'
'Pamela Bowden's distinguished Mme Larina.'
'. . . a beautifully clear Mme Larina – dignified and beautiful.'

Royal Opera House, Covent Garden: Eugene Onegin *(Tchaikovsky)*

'Some of the most satisfying singing came from Pamela Bowden.'

Wexford Festival Opera Gounod's: Romeo and Juliet

'The Nurse, Pamela Bowden, a rich contralto of fine quality, was exceedingly good.'

English Opera Group: Dido and Aeneas *(Purcell)*

'. . . an excellent Sorceress'

Recording: Ruddigore *(Gilbert and Sullivan)*

'. . . a superb Mad Margaret.'

Some Facts and Figures

Pamela Bowden, FRMCM, ARMCM, HonFLCM, FRSA

BBC broadcasts, 1951-1976

Of a total of some 135 broadcasts, a large percentage were performed in London concert halls and churches, the Royal Festival Hall and the Royal Albert Hall (including 12 Promenade Concerts). The list contains major choral and orchestral works performed throughout the UK, as well as numerous Lieder and English Song recitals, contemporary works, first broadcast performances and 25 operas.

Oratorio performances

A repertoire of 52 oratorios by 26 composers.
Of a total of 360 performances:

Handel	*Performances*
Messiah	149
Bach	
Mass in B Minor	31
St Matthew Passion	26
St John Passion	11
Christmas Oratorio	9
Mendelssohn	
Elijah	12
Mozart	
Requiem Mass in D Minor	13
Beethoven	
Choral Symphony, No 9	10
Elgar	
The Dream of Gerontius	16
The Kingdom	10
The Apostles	5
Tippett	
A Child of Our Time	11

Other oratorios performed

Handel
Solomon, Judas Maccabaeus, Israel in Egypt, Jephtha, Samson, Semele

Bach
Ascension Oratorio, Magnificat in D

Haydn, J
Mass in D, Mass in B Flat, St Cecilia Mass, The Return of Tobias, Harmoniemesse, Nelson Mass, Missa in Tempore Belli

Haydn, M
Hispanic Mass (première 1966)

Honegger
King David

Harrison, Julius
Mass in C

Huber, Paul
The Prodigal Son

Mendelssohn
Hymn of Praise

Brown, Christopher
David – A Cantata (première 1970)

Mozart
Mass in C Major

Beethoven
Mass in D Major, Mass in C Major

Bruckner
Mass in F Minor

Buxtehude
The Last Judgement

Cavalli
Mass

Duruflé
Requiem

Dvořák
Requiem Mass, Stabat Mater

Greene, Maurice
The Song of Deborah and Barak

Monteverdi
Vespers of 1610

Szymanowski
Stabat Mater

Schubert
Mass in A Flat

Pergolesi
Stabat Mater

Rossini
Stabat Mater, Petite Messe Solennelle

Verdi
Requiem

Vivaldi
Gloria

Live recitals and concerts

A total of 250 recitals and concerts performed all over the UK as well as overseas (with additional broadcasts).

Conductors include

Ernest Ansermet
Samuel Baud-Bovy
Gary Bertini
Sir Arthur Bliss
Nadia Boulanger
Pierre Boulez
Nicholas Braithwaite
Basil Cameron

Sir Andrew Davies
Sir Colin Davis
Franz Paul Decker
Norman Del Mar
Jean Fournet
Rafael Frühbeck de Burgos
Nicholas Goldschmidt
Sir Charles Groves
Vittorio Gui
Josef Krips
Rafael Kubelik
David Lloyd-Jones
Sir Charles Mackerras
Jean Martinon
Yehudi Menuhin
Andrej Panufnik
Sir John Pritchard
Sir Simon Rattle
Stanford Robinson
Christopher Robinson
Paul Rudhardt
Paul Sacher
Nino Sanzogno
Sir Malcolm Sargent
Hans Schmidt-Isserstedt
Rudolf Schwarz
Constantin Silvestri
Sir Georg Solti
Sir Michael Tippett
Günter Wand
George Weldon
Willem Wiesehahn
Sir David Willcocks
Mogens Wöldike

Index of Names

Readers should note that this index does not include references to the sections *Some Press Opinions* and *Some Facts and Figures,* which are arranged in order for easy reference.

Chapuis, Juliette, 122